# You Don't Travel Alone in Life

## Extracts From My Diaries

# You Don't Travel Alone in Life

## Extracts From My Diaries

*By*

**Dr. E.D. SETTY**

AKANSHA PUBLISHING HOUSE
NEW DELHI-110002 (INDIA)

**AKANSHA PUBLISHING HOUSE**
4649-B/21, Ansari Road
Darya Ganj, New Delhi - 110 002
Ph.: 23263193 / 9811582579 / 09435116718
Fax: 011-23263193
Email: ektabooks@yahoo.com

*You Don't Travel Alone in Life: Extracts From My Diaries*



First Published 2008

ISBN 978-81-8370-156-3



PRINTED IN INDIA

---

Published by Akansha Publishing House, New Delhi and Printed at Aryan Enterprises, Delhi.

*DEDICATED TO*
*MY BELOVED*
*PARENTS*

# PREFACE

The idea of maintaining a diary, noting down the day-to-day events that appeared to me significant simply struck me, soon after my school final in 1948. I have started my diary beginning 1948 and I am still continuing now (2008) with a couple of breaks. These daily noting ranged from a couple of lines to several pages. It is notes to myself and a dialogue within myself and there was no idea of publishing this material, nor anything was written with any idea of possible publication. Only a few months ago, I thought of publishing selections from my diaries whatever may be their worth in the eyes and interest of the readers. The selections from the diaries are reproduced verbatim without any change or editing or with any subsequent status and details of persons and situations that figure in the diaries except occasionally giving some details in parentheses.

The present selections are from 1964 to 2008 spanning over a period of 44 years covering twenty volumes running into some 7500 pages in handwritten manuscript unfortunately, I lost the diaries of the period 1948 - 1963. On my getting the Ford Foundation Scholarship for my undergraduate studies at Gandhigram Rural Institute I left for Gandhigram in 1963 leaving all my diaries and some two hundred books at home in my village. During this period my younger brother Narasing who was staying at the village, ignorant of English language and the value and importance of my diaries and books, sold them away to some shopkeepers as packing material, may be for an insignificant amount of money. As a result, I lost some 15 volumes of my diaries covering my noting of some important events and encounters in my life as a clerk in the State Bank of Mysore (H.O) Bangalore – 1948 – 50, as an Intermediate student in Madras – 1950 – 52 and as a village level worker – 1953 – 63, in the Government of Andhra Pradesh.

The selections in the volume reflect my thoughts, impressions, comments on people, places and books, actions and reactions. I noted down about people, things and events as I felt at that moment. During the period covered in the volume, I have lived, studied, worked at and visited for brief periods several places and countries. In respect to places, they were Gandhigram, my native village, Hyderabad and a few places in different States in India and in other countries. Of countries I visited, they were Australia, Bangladesh, Belgium, Britain, Indonesia, Japan, Malaysia, The Netherlands, Pakistan, Philippines, Republic of Korea, Singapore, Taiwan (Republic of China) and United States of America. The reader will find brief descriptions and comments on people and places I met with and visited. The whole thing is a free and spontaneous expression of my mind without concealing anything and without fear or remorse.

Since the diaries are communication to myself and strictly personal, I have not mentioned the full names of people and their station. There is considerable frequency of family members figuring in my diaries and in order to make their identity clear, I would like to mention their full names and relationship to me.

| | | | |
|---|---|---|---|
| Visal | : | Vishalakshi | wife |
| Pandu | : | Dr. Swarajya Lakshmi | 1st daughter |
| Jeji | : | Geethanjali | 2nd daughter |
| Babu | : | Ravi Shankar | son |

| | | | |
|---|---|---|---|
| Baby | : | Radhika | $3^{rd}$ daughter |
| Kutta | : | Kavitha | $4^{th}$ daughter and the youngest |
| Brother | : | Subrahmanyam | elder brother |
| Narasing | : | Narasinga Rao | younger brother |
| Bujja | : | Jeevaratnam | sister |
| Tiny | : | Manasa | elder granddaughter through my $1^{st}$ daughter |
| Chinna Kutta | : | Poojitha | $2^{nd}$ granddaughter through my $1^{st}$ daughter |
| SSP | : | Sai Srinivas Prasad | $1^{st}$ grandson through my $2^{nd}$ daughter |
| Crystal | : | Chinnu | $2^{nd}$ grandson through my $2^{nd}$ daughter |
| Mahathi | : | Chinbi | $3^{rd}$ grand daughter through my $3^{rd}$ daughter |
| Manu | : | Manu | son of my $3^{rd}$ daughter |
| Meghna | : | Meghna | $2^{nd}$ daughter of my $3^{rd}$ daughter |
| Ammu | : | Anushka Desingu Erram | daughter of my son Ravi Shankar |
| Erram | : | Sai Erram | son of my son Ravi Shankar |

I have used masculine gender in respect to my daughters and my five granddaughters and all my references to them in the diaries. Somehow I am so used to referring to them in masculine gender and I carried out the same gender in referring to them especially the pronoun "HE".

I am aware that some of the persons mentioned in these selections, if they happen to read this publication may have different reactions. I have written what I felt at that moment of writing. It is past and I have no control over it and I cannot retract some of my observations. It is one man's world and how he coped up with situations, endured difficulties and ploughed through life. Some of the readers may find their lives reflected in mine. I leave it to the readers for their impressions and reflections.

**E.D. Setty**

# ACKNOWLEDGEMENT

I would like to record here my sincere appreciation and heartfelt thanks to Sri. K. Murali Krishna who has typed the whole material and prepared the manuscript for publication.

I deeply appreciate my wife Mrs. Vishalakshi for her encouragement while I worked on this book.

I would like to express my thanks and indebtedness to Dr. P. Krishna Moorthy (Professor) for his encouragement and help in my attempt to bring out this publication.

I would like to express my profound thanks to Sri. M.P. Misra of Akansha Publishing House, New Delhi for bringing out this volume.

# ABSTRACT

The selections in the volume reflect the author's thoughts, impressions, comments on people, places and books, actions and reactions. The extracts included in the volume are from 1963-2008. The whole thing is a free and spontaneous expression of the author without concealing anything and without fear or remorse.

Since the diaries from which material is extracted is purely personal without any prejudice and forethought of publication. Some of the readers may find their lives reflected in the author's.

# DECEMBER 01, 1963
# GANDHIGRAM

Touched Jawaharlal Nehru's hand and his shoes, heard him for more then an hour from a distance of 3 yards when he visited Gandhigram on 01-12-1963. This has been a life dream for me, to see Nehru at close quarters and touched him. Held his hand (right) for a few moments. The moment is treasured in a photo taken by my friend K. Krishna Murthy.

**Friday, January 17 1964**

In the morning read a book in the library on 'Reading'. It tells that reading has three aspects: information, inspiration and sublimation.

In the evening read the Biography of John F. Kennedy by James Macgregor Burns. Read the book upto Jack's joining Harvard, the Kennedy family moving to the States from Southern Ireland in the middle of nineteenth century on account of potato famine, the old Patrick Kennedy settling at Boston, his political life and his son Joseph Kennedy (President Kennedy's father), his swift rise in the financial world, President Kennedy's childhood and schooldays, JFK writing his, 'Why England Slept Just at the Outbreak of the Second World War', a graduate thesis, later published. Kennedy then was only 23 years old. Joseph Kennedy, becomes ambassador during F.D. Roosevelt's presidency. JFK later joins navy in his forties.

**Friday, January 24 1964**

Read in the *Encyclopaedia of Britannica* about – David Garrick (1717- 1779) a pupil and contemporary of Dr. Samuel Johnson.

For some time now, I have been reading in, 'Man in the Beginning' by William Howells which deals with some interesting accounts especially of Orangutans, Gibbons, Chimpanzees, Gorillas and Monkeys, the formation of societies and the development of language, the symbol of thought conveyance. Further, in the same book it is interesting to read about humanoid, anthropoid, man-apes, the Java man, the Peaking man, the Africa man and the slow advent of man on this planet and his gradual growth.

**Saturday, January 25 1964**

In man in the beginning read about 'honoured, anthropoid-man apes, the Java man, pekin man, the Africa man, the slow advent of man on this planet his gradual growth.

Another interesting book I have been read for the past four days is "The United States (of America) Political System and How it Works" by D.C. Coyle. It describes the system of the government, of various Political and Administrative Organs, the Federal – State Relations, the Executive, the Congress, the Senate, the Judiciary, the Parties and in a nutshell the American way of life, Political, Economic and Social.

**Tueseday, January 28 1964**

Read in man in the beginning about Paleolithic, Mesolithic and Neolithic stages of man, the hunting tribes of South Africa, the Bushmen of Australia and their peculiar marriage customs, the taboos and their totems, the domestication of cattle, sheep etc., the first raising of grains (crops). The Bushmen are still alive and almost in the same state hunting with those crude weapons of spears, bows and arrows, poison arrows, boomerangs etc. Completed reading the U.S. Political system who it functions.

Read a short biographical sketch of 'Plutarch' (40-120A.D.) a Greek who wrote the lives of Greek and Roman heroes.

Read in the Encyclopedia Britannica about 'Sex, and sexual behaviour in insects, fish, mammals, birds, chimpanzees, apes, monkeys and human beings and of matings, of these beings.

**Wednesday, January 28 1964 29 1964**

Read in the 'Man in the Beginning' about the origin of farming and the evolution of white and colored races, the latter being preponderant in the tropical jones. In certain basic things, such as sex, and behaviour insects, animals and human beings do not seem to differ much.

**Tueseday, January 30 1964**

Today received a letter from Devasahayam. A tragic news. He writes that Malathi, died last month at Kalahasti, he says that she died after her husband giving her an injection as usual for her asthma, some thing has gone wrong which has proved fatal. Malathi was my classmate in V and VI form at Sholinghar, daughter of Rajaratnam. After school days, met Malathi with brother accidentally at Chowdepalle some where in '59-60'; that is after ten years. There she was a teacher for a few months.

**Friday, January 31 1964**

In the afternoon met Miss Padma Isaac, our English teacher. Requested her to clarify certain doubt in answering some questions in 'Socrates' by the way of discussion over Socrates, I just entered over other topics, Enquired of her place and her service in Eluru. She asked me as to how I have developed interest for English literature and what books that I am studying now. 'Man in the Beginning' by William Howard, she queried whether I was interested in 'Anthropology'. I told her that I am interested. There then she gave me a 'Life' publication with illustrations on the origin and evolution of man to read and return.

**Sunday, February 2 1964**

Still with 'Man in the Beginning'. Read about the aborigines of Melanesia, Polynesia, South Africa, of their totems, tattooing, voodoo, tabu, their marriage customs, initiation before marriage for boys and girls, their dress, their food and their crude agriculture.

**Monday, February 3 1964**

Studied a few pages in Man in the Beginning' and some through the introduction in the 'Epic of Man' Life publication. The illustrations are interesting the drawings based on the archaeology, fine reconstructions of the prehistoric life of man.

**Tuesday, February 4 1964**

Studied in the Encyclopaedia of Britannica the short life – sketches of Henry Havelock Ellis (1859 – 1939) a great sex psychologist and the author of the classic, 'Studies in the Psychology of Sex', running into seven volumes and of Ingersoll, American lawyer, politician, writer, an anti-orthodox who fought against traditional Christian belief and faith, a great man in rhetoric, a radicalist and a rebel of religion.

**Tuesday, February 18 1964**

Completed reading a book 'Crime and Punishment in Ancient Society' by Bronislaw Malinowski. It deals with a particular aboriginal tribe Trobiand N.E. of New Guinea in pacific, commonly called as Malenesia. It is anthropological study and mainly deals with the civil and criminal tribal laws, sorcery, witchcraft, suicide and black magic, group sentiments, laws of exogamy, incest.

**Sunday, February 23 1964**

It is something funny. Even without knowing the Hindi alphabets and not even touching a single book prescribed, I sat for the 'Hindi Prathamic' exam. I simply laughed at the situation. The exam was from 10.30 AM to 1 PM. Simply out of my memory, a few words which I have heard in the course of learning to read words scribbled something. It would be a miracle if I get a pass in the exam. At the most I may get about 10 marks.

Perhaps, this would be the first exam in which I will fail. Nothing serious, but technically and academically it would be a failure.

**Monday, March 2 1964**

I must note down here an important habit to me. Smoking has been a source of pleasure and pain since 1944. I enjoyed it and suffered from it. At times, having no money to purchase cigarettes, the habit, the urge has driven me to most delicate, awkward and embarrassing situations. By a conservative reckoning. I would have smoked 1,00,000 cigarettes and beedies ant it would have cost me about Rs. 25,000/-.

**Saturday, March 14 1964**

Received a most moving and pathetic letter from brother (Hyderabad). His description of his economic position, his domestic condition, his most agonized penniless state makes my blood cold. I feel guilty. D. Venkatratnam proved himself at brother to be the meanest and a foul fellow. He has shown his ingratitude. Brother could not return Rs. 20% borrowed from him. Brother wrote that this ungrateful fellow pestered brother for his money without the least realization of the help and hospitality he enjoyed at us.

By now I had about Rs. 60/- when I received the letter. In the afternoon sent to brother Rs. 60/- by T.M.O. wrote him a letter that I shall manage Rs. 600/ for Narasing's marriage. Brother's letter curdles my blood. I am prepared to offer my life to brother. I must be frugal in the use of money and keep the family, do service to my blood and better die doing so.

## WEDNESDAY, MARCH 18 1964
## GANDHIGRAM

In James Thurber's Alarms and Diversions' read on pain, Americanization of some English words and some Crime cases. Highly interesting and humorous.

**Sunday, June 14 1964**

Dr. G. Ramchandran, Director of Gandhigram Rural Institute, an eye witness of all that followed Nehru's demise, till his ashes were immersed in Sangham at Allahabad gave a vivid and moving account, as how people in millions thronged to have a last look at Nehru on his death bed. It was an opportunity to have a first hand account of the gloomy and dark hours of New Delhi on Nehru's demise. Nehru was the essence of humanity. He was the greatest and highest possibility of a human being and of the whole creation. He was a Karma Yogi. He lived true to the principles expounded in the Bhagavad Gita. He combined in himself the science and the art of life. He was humanity and was, in my view, so near to the conception of God. Immortal Nehru.

It is said that Nehru's cremation was the greatest of cremations that history has witnessed, attended by millions and mourned by millions. One age has passed away with Nehru.

**Monday, June 15 1964**

Today, in the English grammar class, wherein we had class work, Prof. Padma dictated to the class a passage for converting it to reported speech. To my utter surprise, the passage was from my letter addressed to her on Nehru's death. I took down my own passage for reported speech. An interesting thing. I felt rather elated.

**Sunday, June 21 1964**

Started reading Dr. Samuel Johnson's the lives of the poets volume - II; read a few poems on Jonathan Swift.

**Friday, June 26 1964**

Completed reading Johnson's life of swift and of Richard Savage disowned by this mother from the hour of his birth, most inhuman and unmotherly instance in history. Savage died in the gaol in 1745. A horrible life marked with freaks of genius.

**Friday, July 3 1964**

Completed reading 'Richard Savage' in Johnson's lives Savage died in the goal in 1745? A humble life marked with freaks of genius.

**Wednesday, July 8 1964**

Received a letter from Visal (wife) that she was dead anxious to see me. She writes that Pandu when asked to go to the nursery, the child says that he would not go to the nursery, but would only attend the school that his father is attending (Gandhigram Rural Institute). He is my beloved spirit with tremendous love for me (that child now is a medical officer).

**Saturday, July 11 1964**

Completed reading a short biography of 'Albert Einstein'. Though it is only a short and hurried biography, it is interesting. On several occasions while plodding through the simplicity of this genius I smiled to the point of shedding tears. The greatest scientist of all ages.

**Monday, July 27 1964**

Received a very painful and disinteresting letter from Narasing, the first letter written in his own hand. His heart speaks. He says that his in-laws have demanded that sister Bujja should be kept separate in the house and only on that condition, they would send their daughter or keep their daughter in our house.

It is a bombshell, a most annoying thing I receive in my life. Sister is our goddess; we are guilty of having neglected her. We will not be worthy of her wisdom and character, even if we sacrifice our lives. A living deity of our family. We cannot keep her separate. At best, she could remain away from cooking etc.

Narasing says that his wife is at present at her mother's, Chittoor and that he would bring her back after 20 days. He seeks my advice. He is my blood, innocent boy. We care for our sister. As it is, the new girl must adjust and accept sister in the house, other wise she could very will remain at her mother's permanently.

**Wednesday, September 2 1964**

Just glanced through once T.S. Eliot's 'Qurtets' four poems in one. Just a superficial reading. Parts of it are beyond my comprehension. His ideas appear so near and at the some time so remote in understanding them. He treats the whole world and the millions of things in it as one. No time for him, past, present or the future. Time is eternal.

## SUNDAY, SEPTEMBER 6 1964

## GANDHIGRAM

A junior student at the Institute has approached me to help him with a summary of the story of Nilokheri by S.K. Dey. This new township is the genesis of Community Development

Program conceived, delivered and fostered by S.K. Dey as a rehabilitation centre of refugees after the partition of India in 1947-1948. I have gone through the book. The languages is masterly, it is poetic prose, pregnant with original ideas. Dr. S.K. Dey, a PhD in Sound Engineering from Michigan State University is the architect of Nilokheri, the mastermind of CD program and the guiding star of extension.

In the Sunday Standard of the Indian Express, read two articles on Indian Ancient democracy. In one article, the author says that India in ancient times spread peace and the impact of her culture, religion and language have a lasting effect on South-East Asian countries – China, Indonesia, The Philippines, Malaya and Ceylon (the names in currency at the time of this entry) and former Indo-China and that India's contact with these countries has only enriched their native cultures, languages etc., but not undermined and extinguished as in the case of European colonial powers which in the name of Christianity and conquest have completely rooted out the Peruvian, Mayan, Mexican and West – Indian cultures – an irrecoverable loss to the world.

**Saturday, September 12 1964**

Received a letter from Dr. S.K. Dey, Union Minister for Community Development & Co-operation, New Delhi, a reply to mine dated 6th September.

The letter is so touching and he expresses his heart and philosophy of life, how he is placed on the citadel and a very testing, difficult and responsible position in the program. He feels when he could come out of this and find time and record all his experiences in the program as he did in the case of Nilokheri. He writes that the has never bothered about himself or his family, neglected his own affairs, and even family too. It is really surprising to learn from the letter that he never had a photograph taken along with his family, and to he says that he would be very happy to send me a photo with his family if he happens to have one (it never came).

A beautiful letter, a piece of literature which is imbued with the philosophy and the truth of life. I treasure the letter.

**Thursday, October 1 1964**

A very tragic tiding. The last flame of the old order (male side) in our family Rajagopal uncle passed away on September 24th at 7.30 PM at our village.

Received this most sorrowful news from my younger brother Narasing today. The irony of the fate is that none of us three brothers was there at the village when uncle passed away and cremated. Narasing says that he received word through a messenger sent from the village while he was at Chittoor, the next day. By the time Narasing reached the village the body has been cremated.

While he was in Bangalore, before he was admitted in the hospital, he asked me to get him a penknife, a sweater old or new, but timid and foolish I was, I could not satisfy his wish. The penknife, I could have, but fate had decreed that I should lament like this now. As for the sweater, there was one of mine at Visal's at Banglore and I asked Visal for it, but those two narrow – minded fellows, Visal and her father refused in my giving the sweater to my uncle, when he was admitted in the hospital in Bangalore. An inhuman and unsympathetic behaviour of those two I have endured. My late uncle complained to me as a child that he could not stand the chill weather in Bangalore. Have I had any money with me, I would have met his need, by buying him a new sweater.

I could not even pay him a last visit when I left Bangalore on 26th August 1964, due to my illness and empty pocket. I hoped then, that he would recover and gain his normal health.

Even the letter I wrote him addressed to the village begging pardon from the dying man, he did not live to see it. Dear uncle I offer to you my silent prayer – your all pervading spirit is the witness to my agony. May your soul rest in peace.

**Friday, October 9 1964**

Seminar on "New Thinking on Gandhian Constructive Program". Dr. V.K.R.V. Rao, Member, Planning Commission of India, a great Economist spoke on the above theme. He spoke wonderfully well. His speech was original, scientific, analytical, practical and profoundly a learned one. In his speech, he blended the Gandhian constructive program with hard economic facts, and showed a new way towards the constructive program.

During the 14 months I have been on the campus of Gandhigram Rural Institute, Dr. Rao's was the best, original and thought provoking speech I heard.

**Sunday, September 19 1965**

Since yesterday I have been going through an interesting book on Abnormal Psychology by J.D. Page of Temple University.

Yesterday read an article on Bhagavad Gita in the September 15th issue of Caravan by one C. Vedarthi (who I later learnt belongs to Arya Samaj). He calls Gita a meaningless thing leading to idolatry. While reading this article at the institute's library, I became rather agitated and emotional and could not stand this criticism on Gita. So, this morning I approached Prof. R. Srinivasan (Chota) and mentioned to him about the critical comments made on Gita by the author of the article. He explained to me as to how the Arya Samajists consider all epics, including Bhagawad Gita as inferior to the Vedas that led to idolatry, and that Arya Samajists depend on Vedas and hold them as sacred. He tried to explain as how the primitive man and most of the religions postulated God as a hypothesis on which they try to solve all the mystery and inexplicable phenomena in nature.

The professor lent me a book – "the Varieties of Religious Experience' by Willam James, the famous classic on the psychology of religion.

**Monday, October 19 1964**

I am glad that I received a reply to my letter from Dr. V.K.R.V. Rao, Member – Planning Commission. The letter shows that he was very much touched by my letter and he gives expression to his heart and universal mind. I reproduce the letter below:

| | |
|---|---|
| New Delhi, | Prof. V.K.R.V. Rao |
| 16th October 1964 | *Member – Planning commission* |

Dear Sri Desingu Setty,

I cannot find words which will express my sense of joy that I felt on receiving your letter. Your sentiments and the fine way in which you have given expression to them, have warmed my heart, strengthened my will and increased my faith.

Thanking you once again for your letter.

With kind regards,

Yours Sincerely,

(Sd) V.K.R.V. Rao

P.S.

As regards my language, it is Kannada, but perhaps your can get a better idea of my ties by the enclosed statement which I wrote out causally the other day when somebody asked me about my language.

(From the enclosure)

| | | |
|---|---|---|
| By language | - | Mysore |
| By birth | - | Madras |
| By education | - | Bombay |
| By integrated life | - | Gujarat |
| By occupation | - | Delhi |

By sentiment — India
By reason — World

**Wednesday, December 22 1965**

Wrote a letter to Kakasaheb Kalelkar, a close associate of Mahatma Gandhi and Rabindranath Tagore, expressing my impressions on reading his book 'Stray Glimpses of Bapu'. This little book in the form of anecdotes (numbering 101) lends a direct insight into Gandhiji's life. In my letter to Kakasaheb, I have stated that the greatest truth that comes out of Gandhiji is his consistency in thought talk and deed. The name Gandhiji has become synonymous with the concept of truth. Gandhiji is Truth. Received the following letter from him.

Camp Bombay,

21-01-1966

Dear Sri Setty,

Your letter of 21-12-1965, is waiting for an answer. Of the four sons of Mahatma Gandhi, one Ramdas is alive. I think he stays at Sewagram Ashram, near Wardha. He is very modest and straight forward.

Now about your other question Gandhiji did not believe in possessing private property, personally. He led an Ashram life. He persuaded his sons to renounce all rights in the ancestral property. He did not force them, but coaxed them into doing so. I think he did a wise thing. Hindu family life throughout the country is vitiated by quarrels over ancestral property. Gandhiji did not object to his sons acquiring and possessing private property of their own. Of course he taught everyone to regard one's property as a Trust, and use it for public good.

Those who become practical sanyasis for public service, are expected to be honourable and humble dependents on society. Gandhiji expected and believed that society would not neglect its servants and dependents in their old age.

'The right of inheritance to ancestral property' is a social convention and lasts so long as society recognises it.

One thing I must write to you, although you have not asked about it.

You write "I prostrate before your holy feet etc". I strongly dislike such expressions. Not out of mere modesty.

Ancient society accepted hierarchies of Varna, Caste, Class, Sex and Status. Therefore, our society regarded all Brahmins as the top people and Shudras as the lowest. Males were considered superior to females, employers to employed. All such gradations of high and low must go, if we sincerely believe in democracy and equality of all. The Geeta and Vedanta also say the same thing. Reverence for elders, humility and spirit of service are the best part of any culture. But why parade one's reverence and humility? This has spoilt our social relations and social solidarity is weakened. Non-Hindus do not lack proper reverence and humility, although they may not fall at the feet of all objects of reverence.

These customs have no spiritual significance or origin. They are the outcome of Feudalism. Non-Hindus are not free from these feudal traits, but we must all be able to shed them. I know it is difficult to shed things which are placed before as great virtues and signs of culture. External forms give a long life to internal old antiquated standards. One cannot improve society without changing external forms rigorously.

I know you will take time to comprehend and appreciate fully, all that I have written above. But truth must prevail in the long run.

Yours Sincerely,

**KAKASAHEB KALELKAR**

## TUESDAY, JANUARY 11 1966

## GANDHIGRAM

A heaviest shock. Prime Minister Lal Bahadur Sastri died at Tashkent at 1.15 AM. A simple but a great man, a man left as heir to India by Jawaharlal Nehru. Sastri will go down in history, in the words of President Dr. S. Radhakrishan, as a determined nationalist, a great statesman and a man of peace, who consolidated forces in India in our recent war with Pakistan. A man of great dedication. He died after signing the peace pact with Pakistan at Tashkent at 4PM yesterday.

## WEDNESDAY, AUGUST 10 1966

## GANDHIGRAM

Finished reading Dr. Verier Elwin's autobiography 'The Tribal World'. In the last chapter entitled Elusive Treasure, he pays high homage to India and her culture and religious tolerance. His concept of love embraces both physical and spiritual. He died as a great lover of tribal people and as a real philanthropologist. Though of British origin, he died as an Indian in spirit and fact.

## SUNDAY, NOVEMBER 27 1966

## GANDHIGRAM

The days are simply meaninglessly rolling by. No substantial study except a pleasurable excursion into the mysteries of sex in Ellis (Studies in the Psychology of Sex – 7 Volumes). For several months now, I have been reading Ellis, and today I read some case histories of the development of sexual instinct in man.

"Women for bearing, boys for pleasure and melons for delight"

This is the first instance in a case history of an English man (soldier), who made use of melons and papaya for coitus, which says (rather they are) nearer to the moist vulva, interesting reading of queer ways of satisfying the sexual need.

**Saturday, July 2 1977**

In the evening read a few pages in Clyde Kluckhon's 'Mirror for Man'. I simply love reading this book. It is a beautiful book on Anthropology.

For several months now, I have been observing a group of four mendicants, three men and one old woman. They sleep in the open space on the way to the staircase of the building where we reside (16-2-701/5/11 Malakpet, Hyderabad). During the day time, they go about begging for alms in the Koti area and by the evening they return to their lodge! They simply sleep on the ground. They use some old and tattered clothes as bedding. They appear to have not washed their bodies for years. Even after defecation, they do not seem to wash. They go in heavily soiled rags. After they settle down in the evenings, they begin their unending wrangling. The language they use is raw, vulgar, when it comes to a member in the group accusing another in the group or some relative in their home village. I do not know where they come from and their marital status. They are in their fifties. But one man in the group known as Sayalu, indulges in such vulgarity – the words or abuses refer only to male and female genitals, anus, sexual intercourse, sucking the penis, licking the pudenda, biting the clitoris. He repeats these juicy terms many a time. Last night till midnight this man swam over such a ocean of vulgarity. The group seems to enjoy it.

**Saturday, August 13 1977**

**Jowai**

It has been raining all through the night. Though, I could not visit Cherrapunji, 55 Km. from Shillong, this time, which receives the highest rainfall in the world (around 550 inches) I could have some idea as how it rains all through there. The rainfall here is intermittent – a sudden downpour, drizzle and then clear sky, then drizzle followed by downpour, it goes on in this fashion. When you look at the green hills, the clouds and the sky, while it rains, all things appear as one integral system of nature.

While at Jowai, I had an opportunity of interviewing one Mr. War, a local entrepreneur. The following is the summary of account he gave on the Khasi and Jaintia tribes.

The Khasi and the Jaintia are matriarchal, matrilineal, metronomus and martilocal people. The youngest daughter inherits the property of the mother and she in turn is supposed to take care of the parents. The maternal uncle takes care of his sister's children. In a way, he is the guardian and social father to the children of his sister.

After marriage, the man moves to his wife's residence. In some cases, he is a night visiting husband. He stays overnight and in the morning he leaves for his residence. This system prevailed in Kerala, when the Namboodiri married a Nair girl.

Christianity was introduced among the Khasi and Jaintia a century ago. The first missionaries were the West Presbytarian, later followed by other denominations. The predominant sect is Protestant followed by Catholic. About half of the population here is Non-Christian, unconverted following their traditional belief system and faith. Christianity, as a new religion of the converted has not effected their customary laws and practices, except one change, a significant development of individualism and emergence of nuclear families – a move from joint – extended families.

In the case of the unconverted (we have to use this term since the advent of Christianity in this region), the order predominant is the Joint-Family System. By virtue of the joint-family system with farming and business, the inconvertible are better off compared to the Christian tribal groups wherein in the case of the latter, the tendency is for careers, jobs which also lead to emergence of nuclear families and development of individualism.

The non-Christian tribes as they did for ages, worship Rivers, Forests and Hills. They are nature worshippers as the early Aryans. A river that is worshipped by them is sacred to them and fishing is forbidden from such a river. They consider forest as scared and they used to offer cocks and hens as sacrifice to the forest. These natural resources sustain their life and so they have been deified.

There has been a long drawn feud and incessant battle between the Jaintia and the Khasi during the earlier centuries and it declined after the advent of the British to this region.

Both the Christian and non-Christian tribes in the area are westernized in their food, dress, habits, table-manners and keeping of their houses. This westernization is more conspicuous among the Christian tribes.

The dwellings of these people mostly made of wood and bamboo are simple, neat, elegant and well kept. Each house has a drawing room with wooden & crane furniture and photographs. Photography is a hobby and craze among the young and old of both the sexes.

The elderly women in their dress and manners are westernized. They shake hands with the visitors and conduct themselves as westerners. There is some mix of English among Jaintia. I saw seven men born to English fathers.

Before leaving his home at 6 PM. Mr. War treated us with bread and tea. On our way back to the IB, he took us to his maternal uncle's house. There we met one of his nieces, a spinster, a beautiful, smooth fair complexioned, delicate woman, so soft as a tender banana leaf, a flower with fine fragrance passing as momentary phenomenon. My friend Dr. N.P. Singh got transfixed by her looks. The fellow went on day – dreaming on our way back to the Inspection Bunglow.

**THURSDAY, AUGUST 18 1977**

**TURA – MEGHALAYA**

I feel like describing the weather in Tura, the district headquarters of Garo Hills. The town is surrounded by hills all around. You feel as if you are in a cauldron, on an hot pan, perspiring and feeling miserable. The weather here is killing, most enervating and it is a horrible climate – a contrast to Shillong in the State of Meghalaya. I felt terribly exhausted after interviewing a couple of entrepreneurs. I could not sleep in the night.

**Saturday, October 8 1977**

Prof. Aiyappan was expected to arrive at Ranchi this forenoon from Sambalpur and so Dr. Sahay suggested to me to wait at Hotel Anand to receive the professor. Prof. Aiyappan stayed at the same hotel on 6$^{th}$. While I was waiting for the arrival of Prof. Aiyappan at the hotel, Dr. Sahay called and informed me that he would go to the department direct form his residence and that I take Prof. Aiyappan to the Department of Anthropology. One of the finest and happiest moments in my life was when I saw Prof. Aiyappan arriving on a cycle rickshaw to the hotel. It was a tremendous relief for me. He wanted to have just a wash at the hotel. We had Breakfast together. I explained to him the cancellation of the flight on 6$^{th}$ to Ranchi from Calcutta. I took him to the Department of Anthropology and by then Dr. Sahay also has arrived.

There was no Viva as such. Prof. Aiyappan suggested a few titles that I should read for acquainting myself with theoretical knowledge which should precede my analysis of the Valayar of South India, when it comes to publication. My doctoral thesis advisor did not ask me any questions on my dissertation.

Prof. Aiyappan pronounced congratulations to me, "Dr. Setty, we admit you to the fellowship of Doctorate in Anthropology". I thanked Prof. Aiyappan and Dr. Sahay.

In the evening took leave of Dr. Sahay with a heavy heart. He is a simple, honest, scholarly and a spiritual man. He seemed very much moved, when I took leave of him. Left by train to Calcutta.

## WEDNESDAY, OCTOBER 19 1977

**Hyderabad**

Ralph Waldo Emerson seems to me an institution aggressively individualistic. His essays contain precious pieces of wisdom and erudition. Speaking of travel, he says – soul is no traveler.

## WEDNESDAY, NOVEMBER 23 1977

**Aizawal – Mizoram**

A word about the girls in Aizawl – Mizoram. They are strong, sturdy, short with unusually big breasts, quite free in social interactions and hard working. An army man, an informant informed me that in olden days men were mostly engaged in hunting or warfare, inter-tribal or intra-tribal and so it was the lot of the women to sustain the families economically. Now, there is no more of head hunting among the Lushai, which was prevalent in earlier centuries. Otherwise, the customs and practices have not undergone any significant change. Men continue to be lazy and are mostly supported by the women.

Aizawl resembles Kohima perching on hill top amidst beautiful green valleys. But the only problem here is water.

## MONDAY, NOVEMBER 28 1977

**Ziro**

The Apatani and the Nishi, look simple with their traditional dress and headgear. One conspicuous custom among the Apatani women is their nose ring, a blackened flat piece of bamboo driven into the nostrils on both sides, which flattens and pushes down the nose. It makes the face ugly and devilish. They start this operation when the girls are quite young and the women when advanced in age, the flatness of the nose widens and it looks as if it is sticking on to the face as a tissue with narrow nostril holes for breathing. Minus the wanton aberration of the nose, the Apatani women look beautiful. Though there is move among the younger generation of women (nubile girls) to do away with this custom, there is a counter move to this, advocating continuance of this custom as deterrent to non-Apatani young men who are after Apatani girls. One informant told me justifying the continuance of the custom, disfiguring the nose of the girls as something repulsive to the non-Apatani including the men from the plains area too.

## WEDNESDAY, NOVEMBER 30 1977

**Ziro to Daporijo**

Daporijo, a small town, sub-divisional headquarters is situated in a valley surrounded by high hills with luxurious vegetation. People here who live in small scattered settlements mostly on hill tops consider the small town Daporijo as a city. Back to Ziro after the work in Daporijo the next station is Along 165 Kms from Ziro. During the entire drive of 165 Kms birds are a rarity. I saw one Kite and another black bird resembling a crow. Monkeys are absent. I had a glimpse of large sized black squirrels, a couple one chasing the other.

The weather is pleasant, cool and an aroma blows around you gently.

**Monday, December 26 1977**

Back to the Institute, Hyderabad after 44 days of research work in the North Eastern States. A memorable day. My beloved adviser Dr. K.N, Sahay has sent me the official communication on the award of PhD. His covering letter is so moving especially "now be on your own. It ends my responsibility". A kind and generous man. I am ever thankful to him.

## WEDNESDAY, SEPTEMBER 6 1978

**Hyderabad**

It is Vinayaka Chathurthi, (Ganesh Festival). It was celebrated at home. Visal as usual prepared several items. She enjoys preparing them.

My thoughts flashed back to my childhood days. How important this day was considered, my looking upto this day several months in advance, the preparations, getting up very early in the morning for collecting fruits & flowers, the religious fast until puja and in the mean time looking for snacks like pelapindi (roasted rice flour mixed with jaggery and made into small balls) and panakam (sugared water with lemon juice and cardamom). Oh, how the day was celebrated! That seems to be altogether a different life, not to experience again. It remains a dream, a sweet dream, a reality experienced for several years in my childhood until I completed my primary school. A lot of change now, not only in me but in the present generation of children. With this reminiscing could not sleep until 1.00 AM.

**Saturday, October 21 1978**

It was a telegram from Bangalore, informing that father-in-law (T. Ayyaswamy Setty) passed away at 4 PM today. The telegram was given by a neighbour.

Father's-in-law long journey ended today. I think, he was around 85 years.

He was individualistic by nature, man of immense self confidence, which appeared sometimes as self-conceit. He was never in the habit of consulting others, seeking opinion of others. He did things on his own. His relationship with relatives was narrow. He never bothered about people beyond his own family. He loved his daughter (Visal) with all intensity. She was all affection and love for him.

He was terribly concerned about Ramaiah (his second wife's son) despite the knowledge of his conception. A great thing to admire in him. He showed concern to me because of his daughter. I doubt his having had confidence in me. Yet, I am thankful to him for having bestowed on me his daughter who is a blend of strong character, highly intelligent with wonderful organisational abilities, aggressive, adamant, quarrelsome and a born fighter. She will never say sorry. But a loving mother.

Father's-in-law long life ended today. May his soul rest in peace.

**Tuesday, January 9, 1979**

My article on caste re-titled by the editor 'Caste Hierarchy': the crumbling edifice "has appeared in social welfare – December issue, I must be thankful to the editor for her beautiful editing and some pictures included illustrating the article.

## SUNDAY, JANUARY 28, 1979

**Mizoram**

The Mizos are in transition. They have moved from a subsistence, self-contained economy to monetary economy with increased dependency on others. They seem to be drifting and losing their traditional moorings. There does not seem to be any comprehensive economic program for them. Most of the officials working in Mizoram are outside the territory. Mizoram as a Union Territory is centrally administered. A total new approach to their economic development in needed.

**Wednesday, February 7, 1979**

In the evening had a late phone call from N. Reddeppa Reddy met him at 7 PM at a hotel opposite to the secretariat along with PN Reddy. I was meeting him after eleven years. He was responsible for my selection for DRS at Gandhigram. We had some drinks. He introduced to me one Shunmagam PA to N. Amarnath Reddy, Minister for Cooperation.

**Monday, February 19, 1979**

I was taken aback and shocked when Subbanna, the steno typist attached to me and Akhouri told me coldly that in case he were to type personal letters, he will mention that in his official diary submitted to the Secretary, that both Akhouri and me have been giving him a lot of personal work. I should have taken back the letter I have given him. As a kind of obligation he did two letters to Prof. Sol Tax and Syril BelShaw, Canada. Later in the afternoon I mentioned to him with all caution and frankness that he can show the personal work under O.T to which proposition he pleaded his uprightness. I take him as he is. This interaction with him troubled me a lot. I think (rather heard him sharing with another person) he had attended an interview this morning and may be he has a chance of settling in a new job. He styles himself as straight as a foot ruler. Ok let him enjoy his uprightness.

**Saturday, March 3 to 16, 1979**

Left for Ujjiain on 6$^{th}$ night and stay at Ujjain till 10$^{th}$, and back to Bhopal on 15$^{th}$ morning and to Hyderabad on 17$^{th}$ morning.

An interesting thing to note in this trip is about my companion on the tour. He is a first rate glutton, devoted to eating and the second is films. He has terrible weakness for a variety of food items. He makes plain of his gastronomous interest. He eats with such acidity. He is intelligent but immature. Wants recognition from others. He is unbelievably impatient and makes a poor fool of himself. He took pretty care of me on the whole a dependable man.

During the tour bought living Wallace' the three sirens and completed reading it and another Roots by Alex Haley I wanted to read both the books.

**Wednesday, April 4, 1979**

A very sad day for me. Around 12.30 PM heard that Z.A. Bhutto was hanged in the morning. I mourn his death. In my entire knowledge of Muslims in history and through personal information, the only man I admire was Bhutto. He has become history, a martyr. It is a hero's death at the hands of a dictator. It is a triumph for Bhutto and a tragedy for Pakistan. The thought of Bhutto's death at Gallows haunts me. It is personal tragedy to me. Bhutto will ever remain in my memory.

**Tuesday, May 1, 1979**

In the afternoon, after lunch read Sai Baba Avatar upto 3.30 and tried to have some nap. I went to sleep with some thoughts of Sai.

I had two dreams. In the first I saw some unknown to me driving motor bicycle at neck breaking speed at Abid's turning. It appeared as the road leading to Koti from GPO. I seemed to be moving fast along with him. In continuation to this I saw a lioness, let free running towards me. The location appeared to be near a railway track. I jumped for safety. I was so scared that the beast will pounce on me and kill me.

In the second dream, I appear to be near a blackboard, I write something on the board showing and vehemently observing that villages have been neglected and the villages were not developed as per their wants and needs of the villages, that they were not taken into account. I appear to be sharing this with a Youngman. Another person is also there. Their faces appear. In order to stress my point I say that I have 30 years of experience with village work. At this point of time the Youngman pressed his hand, the fingers pressing both sides of my forehead. Immediately, the person appears to be Sai I feel a vibration in my body. The whole body turns like hot gas, it loses its corporeal nature, I feel some energy. So powerful permeating my whole body. I shout Para Brahmam and immediately remembering it was Sai who was doing so say Sai Brahmam, I struggle to get out of that state.

I don't know whether it is fantasy, wish fulfillment – the residue of the day's work.

A few minutes after I woke up GVS, knocked at the door and told me that he was going to his uncle's. At the same time he handed out to me a postal envelope. Though I was telling him that I needed one, I did not expect it at that hour. I thought I should use it for the letter I have been planning to Sai Baba. After tea at 5.30 drafted and posted the letter to Sai Baba.

Here is a copy of it.

Dear Sri Krishna Sai,

In my first visit to Prasanti Nilayam last December, I had your darshan, but lacked the strength to touch your divine feet at the mandir. Grant me strength to touch your feet. Bless me with your grace to experience that divine spark. I often suffer from fear of death. My goal is union with Brahman. Meanwhile desire to visit the USA or Canada to do my post doctoral work and earn some money for my five children and give me strength to love all.

Earnestly seeking your blessings.

**Friday, May 4, 1979**

In the evening went to Sharma's. He received us kindly. Saw in some of the publication 50th birth anniversary saw one picture of Sai's mother and father offering puja to him.

Of all photograph of Sai, one in black and white of his 50th birthday November 23, 1975 is extremely beautiful and I see Satyam, Sivam and Sundaram in that. It is God's face of my imagination.

Can Sai, get through me, grace me with a spark of divinity. I crave for that.

**Thursday, June 7, 1979**

(I have been an intern in a two week sensitivity training at Hotel Harsha – Bangalore).

A significant day. In the Systems Processes Analysis Laboratory, I had my turn in narrating to the group about my primary system (family) and important events in my life. The facilitators in the lab discovered for me phenomena and causes which were totally out of my consciousness. My position in the primary system was subordinate status. I have been replicating the same subordinate behavior in every situation. The emerging and revealing things are:

1. Uncle and Granduncle were the authority figures. I did not encounter them directly. I made use of aunt (Perumganji, wife of my granduncle) as a medium.
2. Father and mother played a subordinate role in the family. Father had no role in my education. I find myself doing the same thing in respect to my children. Mother took care and was concerned about my education and the same thing my wife is doing now.

3. I have internalized my father's subordinate role and non-interference in the affairs of others.
4. I had no contact or relationship with my elder brother as a child, the same sense of distance continues now, though we love each other.
5. My attempts for my formal education appear to be a compensatory behaviour. The reasons for organizing and running adult literacy classes and pial school for children are thought to be what was denied to my parents. (Both were illiterate).
6. I should redefine my work system and the entire environment in terms of reality and act.
7. I should acknowledge my strengths and positive things.

**Sunday, June 10, 1979**

Sent a telegram and a letter to Visal that the chain was found at the village and it was stolen by Murali. They will have a relief and be happy.

Pulin Garg beautifully discussed the Indian tradition in terms of its philosophy, social structure and personality structure/value. He is an institution by himself.

My lovely number is 9. I tried to work out my longevity as I understood what Peter Vidal has written in the Sunday standard. I may live up to the age of 88, is upto 2012 AD.

**Sunday, June 24, 1979**

Completed reading 'Roots' by Alex Haley – a moving and absorbing saga on the institution of slavery. Babu (son) read parts of Roots and wept over the way, the human individual, captured, purchased and huddled in boats and treated as subhuman by the so-called civilized white man. A shame to the history of mankind.

**Monday, December 3, 1979**

Brother (elder) rang up and informed me that sister has written a letter that mother is sick, stopped taking any solid food, just takes some liquid and talks in a confused way. Met brother in the evening at his office and read the letter.

Mother has been a Karma Yogi all through her life. She suffered much for the past thirty years, since the partition of our joint family in 1947, she has no proper food and clothing. Narsing has been partly a cause for this situation and mother's suffering. Narasing continues drinking.

Mother has no sheet to cover during the nights. During our visit to the village we have taken two sheets with us. I asked Visal to give one to mother. But heartless she was, she did not. I would have given one, but I tried to avoid an ugly scene between Visal and me. Visal has been all through vigilant, suspecting that I may secretly manage to pass on some money to mother, sister or Narasing. Her suspicion was correct. I have concealed one- hundred rupee note inside a wrapper of a book and I managed to pull it out and passed it on to sister.

**Saturday, December 15, 1979**

Met P. Chegalvaraga Setty who is in his eighties. He has lost his sight. He has a beautiful memory. He looks like a rishi.

Kaviah with whom I have been close died on 4$^{th}$ December. It is said that he fell at Kothabavi and on the third day he died. He was ninety. A strong character highly individualistic. He loved cows and dogs more than people. He was a bachelor, feel sad over his death.

**Sunday, December 16, 1979**

I think after over 30 years I visited Chinnakonda Visal, Narasing, Narasing's younger son Sriramulu and Murali were in the group. A larger number of people visited the temple. The interesting feature was the Harijans' visit to the temple, a freedom denied to them for centuries.

**Tuesday, January 8, 1980**

The little fellow dances to the tunes of songs from the radio – his jerks, twists and the rhythm he maintains are just beautiful. I wonder, how he has learned and developed this aptitude for dance. It seems to be a natural gift or he inherited his father's interest and liking for dance?

Baby too does, but he is more sober, his is one kind of fineness. All the five children are gift of God. All are beautiful. May God help them grow well and become good citizens.

**Thursday, January 31, 1980**

A tragic news from the village that Middinti Pairu Chengalvaraya Setty passed away on 23-01-1980. Exactly a month ago on 22-12-1979, when we visited the village, we visited him and took leave of him. He looked serene with his Naam (a religious mark on the forehead) with this usual buoyant self and cheerful smile. He wept with deep emotion that he may not see us again. I never thought that he would pass away so soon. While taking leave of him, he made the following observation in a deep emotional tone – tears rolling down his cheeks.

1. That Grandfather (Venkataswamy) was a God to him – they endeared each other.
2. He did not commit any sin except his pre-marital and extramarital relations.

He means so much to me right from my childhood. He has been much in my psychological realm. He has been a significant member in the village. I remember him for his lengthy stories. He was a great story teller. During those days, his stories running sometimes over one hour was a source of entertainment and pastime during summer nights. I remember him reading Bhagvad Gita and recitation of Anjineya Dandakam (enumerating the divine qualities of the deity Anjineya) – his short-stint and stay in Bangalore and his pilgrimage to Benares and other holy places in South India. He died childless though he went for a second marriage for a child. His second wife ended her life by suicide. His first wife Janaki remains a lonely widow. He was one of the symbols of the village, a simple, but an understanding and noble gentleman. A memorable generation has passed away with him. Middintiaayana was known for his knowledge of Hindu epics and puranas, his choice was Kishkindacanda (canto) in Epic Ramayana. I mourn his death. May his soul rest in peace.

**Monday, June 23, 1980**

A tragic end of Sanjay Gandhi in an air crash today at 8.12 AM along with one Saxena. Mr. Gandhi had a meteoric life, at the age of 33. A courageous man, had high talent in organising the youth, quick and bold in decision making.

**Tuesday, June 24, 1980**

The tragedy continues by morning V.V. Giri died in sleep.

**Monday, September 15, 1980**

On the invitation of Institute of Engineers (India), AP. Centre attended their 13th Engineers day. For the first time heard Mr. M. Channa Reddy, Chief Minister. He spoke well. He was followed by Dr. Ram K. Vepa. He delivered Sri. M. Viswerarаya lecture. It was on small industries, a comprehensive coverage. It was 7.20 PM when the function ended. It was a group of experienced old and young engineers. An intellectual group. It was interesting to see some of the retired engineers. Same dotting aged with wisdom and experience.

**Sunday, October 20, 1980**

It is a holiday. Came to the Institute to attend to some drafting of letters. There were several others also who had come to the Institute around ten in the morning chanced to meet Mr. Raghu in front of my room. On my greeting him he shot at me a painful unwarranted question "why are you haunting the Institute". I just mumbled that I had some work to attend to. I could have retorted in the same tone, put him the same question, but I restrained myself.

His style of dealing with people in unsavory. He is alienating the staff in the Institute. At this point of time, 30 days since he took over, he has proved his incompetence.

**Wednesday, January 7, 1981**

An obituary note on Moti.

I record here with all sorrow the tragic end of a dog who has been named 'Moti' after the name of the place, where we live Motinagar, which again got its name after one Lambadi Motilal, the original resident of the locality.

When we moved to Motinagar, there was a pack of dogs, young and old. In the beginning three fellows started attaching themselves with us. Of the three, one was Moti, the other two gradually dropped out and Moti identified himself with us, and we reciprocated his attachment. He lived with us for five months.

Right from the beginning I sensed that there was some special, fateful relation between him and me. He was in his youth, silent, grave, dignified and peculiarly he had the looks of Modoku of my village. He had a special attachment to me. In respect to the other members in the family though they used to feed him he had some distance from them.

For the past one week, he had been suffering from breathing trouble. I know he will not live long, but could not do anything. As fate would have it I missed seeing him this night. He did not eat any food today.

At 12 mid night when Visal and I came out, I saw Moti lying down in front of the house, out side the fence. I felt his body, it was cold. An end to a kind of an eternal friend. He was given a simple burial nearby. I pray for his soul and pray to him to forgive the lapses on my part.

Moti will ever remain in my memory.

## THURSDAY, JANUARY 15 1981

### Hari's Death

I should say, it was fateful, that after Moti's death, Hari's followed little Hari was ill for a week. We took him to vet several times. He was treated but the end came at 10.30 PM on 18th. He was alive till children and Visal returned from the T.V. an hour before his death, he looked at me with his parting looks and shed tears. I feel that he had something of fateful or Karamic relation with me.

The whole family mourned his death. By 11.30 PM, we buried him close to Moti.

Hari remains in our painful memory. He will live with us so long we live. I pray for Hari's soul.

### Tuesday, January 26, 1982

For a few days now I have been reading Oscar Wilde. Completed reading his Gaol Memories 'De Profundis'. To me it is a master piece from a great genius. His language, the idiom, the ideas, the deep sorrow that he was afflicted with and the emotions of admiration and love that the book kindles in you should be studied over and over again. Years ago I read his 'Portrait of Dorian Gray', a moving story and a great piece of literature.

**Tuesday, April 29, 1982**

A session to a group of 30 medical officers (being trained by the Institute of Administration) - the venue, AP Training Centre, Directorate of Medical & Health Services - Koti) on extension techniques – 4.30 to 6.20 PM. Some of the participants told me that my session of all the faculty was the best and one lady pointed out, that my talk was close to their hearts. I felt happy.

**Monday, May 3, 1982**

Around 10 AM. Mrs. Lakshmi Devi, Project Officer, Women's Development Agency, Medak met me in connection with the institute running the EMD for women of Mahila Mandals in the Medak block. Took her to Principle Director, on her request the fee was reduced to Rs. 20, 000 from 22,500/ -. Action on the programme fell on me. TKC plays the role of a post office. I feel annoyed and irritated over his puppy approaches asking me to do things.

In the course of my talk with Lakshmi Devi, I mentioned my VLW days in Madakasira block. She said she was there as SEO in 1954 then I recalled the person by name Moorsand. She said she is the same person. Obviously she has changed her name. It was a surprise that we discovered each other. We recalled the Madakasira days. She is the first person I met in a programme who has been a contemporary in the block. She left by 1 PM.

**Tuesday, July 6, 1982**

Prof. L.P. Vidyarthi, rang me up from Osmania. Told him that I would meet him at the Hyderabad airport in the evening. Met him at the airport.

**Saturday, July 17, 1982**

Stayed home. I fail to understand the fight among the children. Especially Babu and Baby. They fight like mynahs

No information from Visal. I appreciate the responsibility Pandu takes in managing the home. He is highly capable and an able manager at home. He goes to sleep late in the night after all the tedious chores of cooking, serving and feeding (Baby and the young one). He has no time for his studies.

**Thursday, July 22, 1982**

Pandu did not get up as usual in the morning. We woke him up, but no response, he was not conscious. It was 9.30, we became anxious. We suspected that he had taken some sleeping pills. We hurried him to St. Theresa hospital in an auto in an unconscious consideration. Foolishly I told a nurse that he seems to have swallowed some tablets, they refused admission. While still in the auto he vomited rice.

From there we took him to Dr. Ramnadha Chowdary at Ameerpet CSIET's physician. He too suspected poising. He did not give any treatment and advised me to take the patient to the Osmania.

Hoping that he would be alright. We brought him back home. I cannot explain my anxiety and dreadful thoughts that haunted me. I simply prayed to god to save Pandu's life. Rajeevi was with us.

Even until 1 PM, he did not regain consciousness then we decided that we should take him to Osimania. Meanwhile as god sent one Ranganathan, Divisional Manager, Vijaya Bank, who came to meet me at the Institute, came to the house accompanied by Biswal. He came forward kindly to offer his car. He accompanied us to Osmania. Pandu was admitted to the emergency ward. He was given stomach wash which was an ordeal for him to bear. For a while he regained consciousness, but when asked, he denied having taken any sleeping tablets.

Mean while Rajeevi rang up brother. He came to the hospital around 4 PM. From emergency Pandu was shifted to intensive medical care ward. Here he was examined by a team of doctors. One of them told me that the patient was out of danger, but they were interested in the kind of pills he has taken. And so they took blood sample and urine and brother took these samples to the lab at fever hospital.

Meanwhile around 9 PM, while brother was still in the hospital a police officer rang up the ward and I responded the call. The police has been informed by the hospital that a poisoned case has been admitted in hospital. I informed the police man who called us about brother being at DGP. Later brother informed the police to patch up the thing. Though the police said they would visit they did not I think, the brother's informing them, the police might have made up some story.

Brother left the hospital by 9.30 PM. Rajeevi and I slept in the ward on the floor. My first stay in a hospital in life. I have an aversion for hospital. All thoughts through out the might were on Pandu. While he resting, I often with anxiety observed whether he was breathing or not.

**Friday, July 23, 1982**

Stay in the hospital. Pandu was put on saline and glucose, he has become very weak, and the doctors answered that he was out of danger. In the morning Bujja, Purushtham, brother, Narasmiha Reddy and his wife visited Pandu.

In the evening returned home for a bath. Fortunately Ramanathan met me at the residence and with him came back to the hospital.

In the mid night Pandu, was shifted to a women's ward. The ward was like a choultry where you had every sundry person. It was hellish experience. Pandu had to put up with those conditions.

**Sunday, July 25, 1982**

Pandu was discharged from the hospital. Rajieevi and I took him home by 11.30 AM.

All are concerned and worried about Pandu.

**Friday, July 30, 1982**

Anji asked me to execute a promissory note in his favour for the food material he has purchased and supplied for the marriage plus Rs. 5000/-. We have agreed to give to his son (all around 14 to 15 thousand). My response or reaction was quick. I said it is insulting and humiliating to us to execute a bond for the money and I will not do it. Then Anji said that until the money is paid them, they will not send Kumar with Pandu. I said it was ok. The transaction was business like. Anji played another game. He asked the mediator Muniratnam to take Visal aside (without me) and convince her for the pronote. Though I did not have a chance to tell her what Anji has demanded from me, she too has given the mediator the same answer.

The whole affair the entire process and Anji family's behaviour was disgusting and repulsive. We had to go through this shameful and humiliating ordeal. We had to swallow every shame. In this game played by Anji and his wife, Muniratnam as a well wisher insisted that he would stand surety for us, deposit his documents of his housesite with Anji. I simply turned down the idea and suggestion.

I was even prepared for the annulment of the marriage, because their behaviour and the way they treated us was not befitting an affinal Kin, just a few hours and days after the marriage.

Pandu, Visal and I left for Hyderabad on 2$^{nd}$ August, by bus (7 PM). Anji, his wife and Kumar came to see us off at the bus station. It was a mechanical taking leave of them. I did not look at Kumar at all.

**Sunday, September 26, 1982**

Read two essays of Emerson – History and Self Reliance. Every word in the essay is a piece of wisdom. Emerson, an individual with indefatigable confidence surveying, analyzing and critically evaluating the whole mankind. He is a spokesman of Nature and God, an indestructible man. I gain confidence and inspiration when I read him. In respect to travel, my views tally with Emerson's. He is simple, incorruptible, and lofty, a man of all ages.

**Sunday, October 17, 1982**

In the night read a few pages of the picture of Dorian Gray by Oscar Wilde. Beautiful and authoritative writing, where as a genius, he purveys the facilities and wisdom of man.

**Friday, December 10, 1982**

Met Mrs. Gloria in the afternoon on the eve of her departure to her country. She overcame with emotion, shed tears. She said that she and the TMS group found me knowledgeable and yet humble this she said has been corroborated by other participants of other courses where I had sessions.

**Tuesday, December 21, 1982**

A letter by Kumar, written in bad taste, threatening that if we, Visal and I do not meet Kumar with Pandu on 23.12.1982 at Chittoor, he would marry another girl at Tirumala at 10 O' clock on Friday (24.12.1982). The letter is filthy the demand is for Rs. 10,000/-. It is shocking, we are not prepared to pay them the amount and buy the goodness of Kumar, his father Anji and his mother. We are prepared to face the consequences.

## TUESDAY, APRIL 12 1983

### A feeling of flatness

Suddir was kind enough to drop me at Shakkar Bhavan. Mr. Prakasha Rao Director (Training) of Institute of Administration took me to Mr. Padmanabhan, Commissioner, (met him earlier a couple of times). I had a lighted cigarette on hand and I knew that Padmanabhan is conscious of his status and his IAS and resents smoking. The moment I entered his room, with a wry face remarked "Oh! this civilized torture referring to my cigarette and immediately rang up for an ash tray, while I was going out of the room with an apologetic note, to throw off my cigarette outside. He stopped me. At the same time Prakesh Rao in a low cautioning tone advised me to extinguish the cigarette. I did it. This affair made the commissioner uneasy and with this unpleasant impoliteness on my part he started briefing me about the participants 'PA's to Directors and Secretaries of AP Government', and what damage the previous man (a retired man) (Prabhakara Sastry) has done in the class. He suggested that I may touch on behavioural aspects and motivation in my lecture.

The topic was "Public Relations". There were 23 participants (four women) the class was from 3 to 4.30. It went on well.

### Sunday, June 5, 1983

As a member of an eight member Indian Delegation on Small Industry Development in Bangladesh visited Bangladesh, landed today in Dhaka from Hyderabad via Calcutta. It is my first visit to a foreign country.

### Wednesday, July 13, 1983

Pandu underwent caesarean between 9.30 and 9.45 AM. Female baby 3.600 Kgs in weight. As per the thithi, the child was born in makha nakshtra, 2nd pada meenakshi janmanama & simha rasi.

I was the first to see the child after he was washed and dressed. He looks chubby with puffy cheeks. I felt like naming him – 'Goldie'.

Spent the whole day at the hospital. Children are happy over the new arrival. Now a kind of renewal mother, nursing duty to Visal as a grand mother.

**Thursday, July 14, 1983**

The child was kept in the children ward last night. Pandu saw him on this afternoon may be that he is not that happy that it is a baby girl.

My Pandu has become mother.

Sent a telegram to Anji. A letter to sister.

Second fellow is managing the cooking at home.

**Friday, September 30, 1983**

In the faculty meeting Biss charged me that I have not associated him in the TMS and I was trying to settle some scores with him. I got emotionally disturbed. I told him and the group that I am incapable of working with him. I know him as a man of instant elation and instant depression. When he thinks/finds that things are not profitable to him, he withdraws totally and fights with his depression. A very greedy man.

**Monday, November 21, 1983**

A new chapter in life, the long awaited and eagerly looking forward to appointment order from the president of Asian Institute of Technology, Bangkok, Thailand to hand today.

The appointment initially is for a two year period as a Faculty in the Division of Human Settlements. The children and Visal felt happy and it is a turning point in my life.

**Sunday, January 1, 1984**

Leaving for Bangkok. From morning till 4 PM. I found myself in a peculiar psychological state with tension and anxiety. Left for the Hyderabad Airport by 4 PM. Purushotam, Bujja, their two sons, Dr. S. Sudhakar Rao, P. Sambasiva Rao, Kondaiah, Jayachandra Babu, Chaturvedi, Ravi Chandra came to the airport to see me off.

The flight to Calcutta was delayed for several hours and it took off at 2 AM (Jan. 2). Until this awful hour the whole family including mother-in-law, Kumar and Tiny remained at the airport.

I should note one fatal mishap here. The handbag I was carrying was rather heavy and besides the handbag, I had with me a small soft plastic bag which was all the time slipping from my hand. The way leading to the craft was dimly lit. Along with the plastic bag I was holding the purse in which I had my passport and air tickets were in the plastic bag. On way to boarding the craft, the purse fell down. I did not notice it. As a divine help, the security man standing close to the entrance to the craft noticed the purse falling to the ground, shouted that the purse fell down. I could not make out for a few tension filled seconds what he was saying and whose attention he was drawing. As I moved forward dragging my handbags, he pointed towards me and said that something slipped from hand. I went back and to my utter shock it was the purse that contained the passport, the air tickets and the money. Within I thanked the security man and God for saving me from a miserable situation in Calcutta for my onward journey to Bangkok.

**Saturday, January 3, 1984**

Joined the Asian Institute of Technology as a Faculty.

The food I cook for myself, sometimes in the absence of vegetables and change is monotonous and I have to forcibly swallow some rice and yet the wonder is I am living and moving around. I just supplement my rice and the solo dhal or a vegetable with groundnut and orange.

**Thursday, March 8, 1984**

Reading James Thurber's, Harold Ross biography, New Yorker editor. Interesting reading. By chance came across a book on est.

**Saturday, March 10, 1984**

The vegetables, tomato and the other vegetable, I forget the name of it, purchased last Sunday either have got spoiled or dried up. There was no alternative and I cut those vegetables and prepared a curry. I added an overdose of chilli powder to the curry and as a consequence I had to suffer from abdominal pain and gastric trouble.

To go in for some dishes at cafeteria, the smell of pork, meat and fish is repulsive and prohibitive in terms of price. Only once I dared to go for a cup of Yogurt which cost me Baht 8/-. Just I am not prepared to spend eight Baht for one cup of Yogurt. For the past two and half months since I came to Bangkok, I almost had no milk in my diet. I take black tea and no yogurt or butter milk for lunch of dinner. The situation will be different after the arrival of Visal.

After over 30 years of marriage I discover now that I love Visal, besides the sexual craving, I love her as a person for her devotion to me and her love and care for the children. I am aware of her shortcomings, highly individualistic, temperamental and she never bothers about others, than her children and her husband.

By night twelve, completed reading James Thurber's "Herald Ross" – the great editor of New Yorker. In the course of this reading when I came across the funny way Ross drove the car, when he began learning driving, his awkwardness with machines and tools, I found my own fears in him and a similarity atleast in this respect with Harold Ross. I suspected that he was a scorpion and in the last pages of the book, I find that he was a scorpion.

I think scorpions are not good in the mechanical and technical fields. They are at their best when they deal with human behaviour.

**Sunday, March 11, 1984**

For a few days now, I have been reading Robert Ardrey's 'African Genesis'. It is a scintillating book on birds, primates, insects and fish focusing on territoriality, status, societal organization and protection.

**Tuesday, March 20, 1984**

Read Galbraith's 'Voice of the Poor' essays (Rajaji – C. Rajagopalachari Memorial lectures delivered in 1982, when Galbraith was American Ambassador in India). The essays are macro analyses of Economic Development, how the capitalist and socialist methods as of today do not fit in with the stages and process of development in the poor countries.

**Thursday, March 22, 1984**

One Dr. Ulrich Ratsch of Protestant Institute for Interdisciplinary Research, Germany met me this afternoon and sought my ideas on rural development. The discussion lasted for one hour.

Started reading 'The Death of the Family', by David Cooper wherein his argument is that family is boobytrap, that it mutilates or kills the individual and the family should be dispensed with and the individuals are to be emancipated from it. I totally disagree with the specious argument of the author. Difficult to imagine what made the author to come out with such strange and mad kind of advocacy. Needless to emphasize the indispensable necessity of the family, as a basic and fundamental social institution in view of the distinct dependent nature of human infant for his development as an individual and as a member of a society. Of all the creatures the human infant is the most dependent for his survival, growth and development on the family basically constituting the mother and father. Family is the most fundamental primary system and institution. It is only in the case of human infant, one finds the longest contact between the infant and the mother. The family is the first social institution that has emerged in the evolution of human society.

In this context I remember the story of 'The Wolf Boy' written by Dr. K.M. Munshi, the founder and Kulapati of Bhartiya Vidya Bhavan. The story goes that the wolf boy is supposed to have been abandoned somewhere in the forests of Madhya Pradesh in the infant stage and the wolves have reared the child. When the boy was discovered he was eight year old, walked on fours, could smell meat at a long distance, behaved like a wolf, directly ate raw meat with his mouth not using his hands. He was adopted by Dr. K.M. Munshi when he was the Governor of Uttar Pradesh. Every effort was made to humanize him in the human environment, but he could make little progress and he was able to learn some 40 words which was the result of six years of patient and careful nurturing and training given to him. The wolf boy died at the age of fourteen.

**Friday, March 23, 1984**

Started reading 'The Death of the Family' by David Cooper, where in his argument is that family is a booby trap, it mutilates or kills the individual and the family should be dispensed with and the individuals are to be emancipated from it. I do not agree with him. There is a need for such an institution for the peculiar dependent nature of human development.

**Sunday, March 25, 1984**

Read upto 11 PM. Some pieces in 'Fantastic Zoology' some interesting details about imaginary beings recorded in myths and in the writings of Herodotus, Ovid, Homer, Virgil, Pliny, Franz Kafka and several others. It portrays a queer animal, human, plant, fish and insect world all mixed up benevolent and malevolent.

**Wednesday, April 25, 1984**

Called home – Hyderabad. Pandu had a shocking message for me that 'Papa', cousin to Visal passed away. An unnatural and immature death. She was the only person, whom I loved in the real sense. She influenced me in my early youth for several years before and after my marriage. She was very tender, kind, affectionate, deeply loving who gave her heart to me. She ever remained endearing to me. I hear her voice the way she used to address me as 'maa', during her fragrant youthful days. She never demanded anything from me, all the time tender, kind and receptive. She will ever live in my memory. A sweet person. I pray for her soul.

**Thursday, May 10, 1984**

In the afternoon at 4 o' clock Siri driving the car went to one Durga temple located in Silam road in Bangkok to offer puja to the car. It was Visal's wish and I should call it, her insistence. Dr. Vighneswaran and his wife favored us to be with us on this occasion. It was not possible to take the car close to the temple and puja was performed at the Shrine praying to god to protect the car and safeguard the life of people who drive and travel in the car. Visal as usual was more particular of the ritual part of it.

On return, close to the AIT main gate, performed the puja to the car, hurling a cocoanut to the ground and applying turmeric and vermillion to the head of the car and burning camphor. I played the role as stipulated by Visal.

At this moment I have a feeling, sad, pitying myself that I do not know driving. The car is there, but I have to request some one to drive it for me. I should get out of this dependency.

**Monday, May 14, 1984**

The people of Thailand (ninety percent Buddhist) observe and celebrate today as Vaisaka Puja – The Mahaparinirvana of Gautama Buddha. One striking feature among the Thai is the universality of celebration of the day, the discipline maintained by the worshippers, the reverence they have for the Buddha and his Majesty the King of Thailand and the Royal family. I could see some of these celebrations on the T.V.

This day reminded me of April 1956, the 2500$^{th}$ day (anniversary) of Mahaparinirvana of the Buddha. On this day, I was in Renigunta (near Tirupathi). And my own reading and chanting of three words.

I take refuge in the Buddha
I take refuge in Sangha
I take refuge in Dharma

Is still vivid in my memory even after a lapse of 28 years.

**Thursday, September 6, 1984**

Wearing a suit with a tie for the reception today at AIT centre was a big problem and an uneasy project for me. I do not feel comfortable in new surroundings, with new people and in new dress. Dress, especially when it is not the usual one I wear, I feel uncomfortable. On this occasion Visal served as a moral and psychological support. With some perspiration, I put on the suit and hung around the neck, the already knotted tie. The knot for the tie was done earlier by Abbey (Sri Lanka) one of my students.

At 6.30, evening Visal and I joined the reception at the AIT centre. We were received by President Alistair North of

Asian Institute of Technology. The gathering of the faculty was there already. For a while, I felt lonely in the crowd. Then I met Dr. C.S. Jha (India) and Dr. Nishino (Japan) Vice-President of Academic affairs. Had a little whiskey and returned home.

The suit ordeal was over.

**Wednesday, October 31, 1984**

A terrible and shocking news that today Mrs. Indira Gandhi, Prime Minister of India was shot at by three Sikh body guards close to her residence, causing eight wounds. She was rushed to the hospital, she is reported to be in critical state. I am recording this at Bangkok time 5.10 PM. A courageous and a highly capable leader of the country.

**Thursday, November 1, 1984**

With extreme sadness, I note that Mrs. Indira Gandhi passed away at 3 PM yesterday. I came to know of this tragic end of a great person at 6PM. Yesterday. When I noted yesterday evening at 5.10, I did not know the end and was hoping that she would survive.

It was reported that her body guards shot her some sixteen bullets and the doctors were not able to remove the bullets from her chest and abdomen. She was shot at her residence while she was leaving for her office at 9.30 AM. (Indian time).

A great daughter of a great democratic statesman. I could not sleep last night – all thoughts recurrent on Mrs. Gandhi. She became a Martyr for the cause of unity of India. It was the Sikh militancy that ended the life of Mrs. Gandhi. Religion has turned people nasty. Where is the spiritual side of religion? Any religion that uses violence has no future and it will never redeem the individual and help him attain salvation.

A black day in India.

Nine hours after her death Rajeev Gandhi was elected leader of the congress party and sworn as the Prime Minister. This is a bit consoling.

Rajeev may be the person who peter Vidal has predicted, who would become a world leader.

Indira Gandhi's body, it was reported will be cremated on Saturday.

The assassination led to violent clashes in Delhi and other northern towns and it was reported over 200 people were killed and a thousand wounded. The Hindus indulged in burning vehicles and buildings of Sikhs.

One painful and inhuman behaviour was the Sikhs celebrating the Indira Gandhij's death distributing sweets in London.

**Saturday, November 24, 1984**

I used to imagine earlier for some years, how the European setting and people look like. I had dreams of mingling with Europeans in their countries. It was an extension of my daydreaming. Here I am amidst them jostling and interacting. I just cannot believe I am in The Hague. A dream came true.

As arranged at 10.00 in the morning I had a call from Ge. He said he would come to the hotel and pick me up at 10.30 he came on the dot. He took me in his car to his home. On the way, he showed me the Parliament house, some important buildings and took me to the coast where I saw swift and I winds blowing the sand on to the roads. The Hague is located just on the coast of North Sea. At his home, he introduced me to its three lovely daughters. Had some Dutch cook is and sweet drops. The showed me his garden, and a novel way of pot compost making. I also saw on the pastures nearby a large sized wooly sheep which looked like cows from a distance.

Then Ge took me to some giant department stores so crowded, people on a buying spree for St. Nicholas day which falls on December 5. He told me that St. Nicholas day for the Dutch is for more important then the Christmas.

I saw three individuals playing guitar accompanied by songs for alms. On the pavements.

Big crowds in the lanes and shopping centers all in over coats.

In my suit and over coat arranged by Riekerk through Ge I felt a bit clumsy and uneasy.

Bought Dutch cookies and sweet and salt drops for children. Bought a Sony 9 band transistor for three hundred guilders. A bit expensive, and a tea kettle for 50 guilders and some vegetables.

I am highly thankful to Ge. He took so much of pains and spent so much time for me. He brought me back to the hotel by 3.00 PM.

**Saturday, December 15, 1984**

The seminar of 'Which Models for Community Development' was concluded yesterday. My problem today is to reach Brussels airport on way to London from Charleroi to Brussels by train.

As planned yesterday Dr. Seawall, a delegate to the seminar of American Friends Society joined me canceling his evening flight to London. He helped me in carrying my chief burden, source and cause of misery, my suitcase. While leaving Bangkok, I had stuffed the suitcase with three suits, a tiny rice cooker, some quantity of rice, pickles etc. for self cooking and so the suitcase turned out to be a small whale.

I had an horrid experience at the Brussels airport. While going up on the escalator holding in two hands, the handbag and the devil suitcase, I lost my balance and the suitcase rolled me down on the escalator, my spects fell down and I became totally panicky. It was similar to the frightening experience. I had last year on the roller coaster in the Siam park in Thailand. Dr. Seawall came to my rescue. I managed to save my spects but got my left thigh slightly bruised. I escaped from a major hurt to my body. I cursed myself for unimaginatively stuffing the suitcase. Lesson : travel light.

Arrived London in the afternoon and Mr. Vokes received me and drove me to his residence. Mr. Vokes (Bill) is 72, a widower, Member of British Empire (MBE), a sweet tempered man. His son Dr. Vokes was a faculty earlier at the Asian Institute of Technology, Bangkok. Mr. Vokes, my host now fought in the Second World War and he is very close to Prime Minister Mrs. Margaret Thatcher. By the way, he insisted that I should address him 'Bill'. He lives alone in his house.

**Sunday, December 16, 1984**

Bill took me on a short tour of some popular places in London. He himself drove the car. The tour sitting in the car lasted for 1 hour 45 minutes going around Buckingham Palace, Downing Street, Piccadilly, Trafalgar Square, Bigben, London Tower and River Thames. I have known these places only through the novels of Charles Dickens, Sherlock Homes of Conan Doyal, Oliver Goldsmith and other English writers. Today I had a passing glimpse of these historically & politically famous landmarks of London.

**Thursday, December 20, 1984**

Returned from London via Singapore to Bangkok.

Mother is no more.

Shocked to learn from the letter received in my absence that mother passed away in the village on December 5 and the last rites were fixed for 19th December. It should have been performed yesterday. The saddest and the cruelest part is that I was not with mother in her last moments. But I have noted in my dream I had on December 1, that mother has passed away. It was a premonition. Beg your pardon mother.

**Monday, April 1, 1985**

Received a letter from brother. He sent the amount to sister and asked her to take Narasing to Vellore for examination and treatment. Narasing should recover and live long.

The gastric pain has grown acute. In the evening met the compounder at the medical centre. He gave me some tablets, despite taking them, I had gripping pain last night until 12 God forbid that it is not ulcer leading to operation I dread any operation.

In this condition, I simply think of Visal. She should be with me. But she cannot come until June, April and May are going to be troubled uneasy months.

Last night Abey and Prof. Siriwardene, came to see me.

**April, 16 and 17 1985**

On 16th morning Aris took me to his Centre for Rural Technology Development (CRTD). Nimi joined us there. Some training program was in progress at the centre and I was asked to address the participants. I did and the participants expressed their appreciation. Aris took me around the experimental farm.

He arranged planting of a sapling by me with my name written on a stand planted close to the sapling. That was noble of him. Around 11.30 AM. Aris' colleague Funny drove to Santo Cruz, a small municipal town, 25 K.M. from there to meet Leplay president of a volunteer organization. They briefed me on their activities and on their request spoke to them on community organization. They had arranged lunch for all (16), but my lunch consisted of a few pieces of melon, except rice, every other item was non-vegetarian.

Returned to CRTD. Gloria Martinez, who was a participant in an eight week International Training program on Training Methods & Skills at SIET Institute in 1981 came to meet me and to took me to Manila. She took me to her office. In the simmering heat had some relief in her air conditioned room for a few minutes.

From her office, she took me to the Ministry of Local Self Government. Met Bernadette, Gloria's batchmate in the training at SIET Institute. Gloria introduced me to the Director Cosio. On this day there was one day seminar in session and I was asked to address the participants in the seminar. I gave a brief account of Asian Institute of Technology, Bangkok.

In the evening, considering my Indian vegetarian background, Gloria came up with a proposal that I may take my vegetarian food at an Indian family.

I was introduced to a masculine looking, talkative woman who was with her child aged about 14 years. At the first sight, I could not figure out whether the child was a boy or a girl but later I discovered that it was a girl. I was supposed to have my dinner at this Indian family but I found the woman so rustic, I told Gloria and Bernadette that I would be happy to have some vegetarian food at Gloria's.

Gloria took me to her residence, introduced me to her husband Ed and her children who were present. She has six children. She fried potato finger tips. Ate some rice with fingertips and yogurt.

Gloria as a beautiful and loving sister arranged my stay at her home. The mattress, the bed cover, the pillow covers and the mosquito net were all new especially purchased for my stay at Gloria's. I was really touched by the love and kindness shown to me by Gloria. The following evening Gloria, Bernadette and some of her colleagues bade me farewell at the airport on my way back to Bangkok.

**April 27 to May 13, 1985**

It is a three – week training program for the personnel of the Pakistan Administrative Services held at Pakistan Academy of Rural Development (PARD) at Peshawar from April 27 to May 13, 1985, organized by the Asian Institute of Technology. Prof. Hiran Dias, Karl Weber and myself were the faculty conducting the program.

**MAY 3, 1985**

**Peshawar**

Visited Taxila an 3rd May. Reflections on this place where Ashoka and Alexander the great stayed. Now all in ruins. Visited the museum.

My classes were appreciated and the participants told me, that my classes were the best of the lot.

Sanitation in the city is awful. I had the admiration for the hefty – towering pathans of the area.

During the last three days of my stay read Bertrand Russell's 'The Nightmares of Eminent Persons, and Toynbee's East to West and between Niger and Nile'.

**Thursday, August 15, 1985**

Today is significant it three ways – India's Independence Day, Pandu's 25th birthday and my visit to Indonesia. Just two years ago I had the least idea that I would be visiting Java and other parts of Indonesia. Got up at 5.30 AM. Visal a usual applied Kumkum to my forehead wishing me a safe journey and I took leave of her and the children. Reached Jakarta airport from Bangkok at 2.30 PM.

Disappointed that Satria Amulya and Pandiangan did not turn up to meet me. But the saving grace was, as a response to my old student Sahat's letter to his colleague in Agricultural Research Institute in Bogor, one Saiful was waiting for me at the airport. Bogor is 90 Km. from the airport. He could not decide whether I should stay at Bogor or in Jakarta. Somewhere in Jakarta, he stopped the vehicle in order to consult Sahat's colleague whom I met in the IRRI workshop in Manila. I sat in the vehicle for more than one hour in a humid condition. Finally, he suggested that better I stay in Jakarta for the night. He took me to Wisata International Hotel. I spent a fruitless one hour in trying to find the telephone numbers of Satria Amulya and Pandiangan through the receptionist.

I had the first experience of slowness and confusion on the part of the Indonesians and the receptionist was totally ill informed.

**Saturday, August 17, 1985**

It is Indonesia's Independence Day. It is her 40$^{th}$ Independence Day. I happened to be in Indonesia for two independence days of India and Indonesia.

## TUESDAY, AUGUST 20 1985

**Bandung**

Heard over the B B C in the night that Pythogoras was Vegetarian. The program was on vegetarian food and cruelty to animals. I am happy that I am a total vegetarian. I love animals. God save them.

**Wednesday, August 21, 1985**

Visited the Agricultural Information Centre, one of eleven in the country at Lembang and later the Agricultural In-Service Training Centre. In the afternoon visited Maribaya water falls – a beautiful spot in a valley flanked by high rising mountains with thick luxurious growth of vegetation.

Tasted a fruit the skin of which looks like the scales of Cobra. Its taste is close to jack fruit.

**Friday, August 23, 1985**

As part of my consulting I had to get some information from the Small Industry Development Department at Bandung. I took an Indonesian official from the LIPI office as my interpreter. On our visit five Indonesian officials in a row sat in front of us to explain to us and answer our questions. I do not know whether I should pity or empathize with their language predicament. All five of them kept on smoking for over one hour, perhaps to overcome their nervousness. Two of them were better than our LIPI young interpreter. It was labour pains for the interpreter for each word.

It may be mentioned here that Indonesia is a clove rich country. One can find atleast one clove tree in the backyard or in the premises of every household. The clove's essence is mixed with tobacco and you will have a powerful smell to both the smoker and the non-smokers around and the smoke will have a slightly burning taste of cloves and the taste and smell will last for several minutes after the smoke. These clove essence cigarettes appear to be unique to Indonesia.

**Saturday, August 24, 1985**

Visit to Agricultural Extension Centre of Subang District at Subang and another small centre under Training and Visit system at Kalijati, 60 Kms from Bandung.

The other persons who accompanied me during the visits were Mr. Zoncochia (UNDP – Representative from Italy, Savithri later my student at AIT) and a LIPI official Hoeman Razi.

I enjoyed the rich and terrific scenery of hills, thick vegetation, deep lush green valleys, vast-stretches of tea plantations, a variety of flower plants and a beautiful weather – all nature's bountiful gift to the people here.

On way back, visited a crater (volcanic) may be 1500-2000 ft. deep and with a radius of a kilometer, spewing hot – gas – powerful sulphuric smell in the area. A memorable sight and visit.

**Wednesday, August 28, 1985**

During my leisure moments I went through an English – Bahasa Indonesia dictionary given to me by Zoncochia. I came across 196 terms in use in Bahasa Indonesian which are derivatives and modifications of Sanskrit, Tamil, Telugu, Hindi, Urdu and Persian languages. Until 8th Century A.D. there has been considerable Indian influence on the East-Indies (Indonesia). Even today, we come across Indian names of people and places and most significantly Lord Ganapathi (Vigneshwara) is the Emblem of the Bandung Institute of Technology. On the BIT campus one could see a large number of idols of Ganapathi.

## SATURDAY, AUGUST 31, 1985

**Visit to Darwin – Australia**

On the flight to Denpasar, Bali Island from Jakarta luckily the man next to my seat was one Woekirsari, a Christian who studied in Pune and familiar with India. I entered into conversation with him all through the 90 minute flight. He informed me that he was going with a group to participate in an Asian Seminar on Social services, Government and Youth. Incidentally, he mentioned to me that Dr. Yogesh Atal, Regional Advisor on Social Sciences, UNESCO, Bangkok, was the convener of the conference at Hotel Bali Beach, Denpasar. I felt happy that I would be meeting Atal.

It was a God sent opportunity to me, I accompanied the group to Bali Beach Hotel in the vehicle that came to the airport to pick them to the hotel.

I was happy to meet some Hindu – Bali workers of the hotel. When I was at the reception counter checking in into the hotel a couple of the workers approached me and without asking my identity they simply asked me, recognizing me, of course that I was an Indian, details about Sathya Sai Baba of Puttaparthi. They told me that a large number of Balinese of Hindu faith are devotees of Baba. They were eager to know about Baba. I shared with them what little I know about Baba. They asked me whether I could send them some books on Baba.

I reflected over the Balinese Hindu. Centuries ago they had embraced Hinduism when the Indian influence and contact was high with the East Indies and especially with Bali. I was told that their Hindu ancestors were persecuted by the Muslims in the region and a few survived with Hinduism on the Bali island. The paradox or the amazing thing is that these people have not visited India, but they cling on to Hinduism with almost all the traditions, customs and rituals associated with marriages and other Hindu festivals and ceremonies.

**Monday, September 2, 1985**

In the evening I saw half a dozen aborigines during my short stroll on the roads of very thinly populated Darwin town. The first man was tall, lean with a lovely beard with torn hawai chappals walking, the second man was old with large mustache in the old fashion, deep dark, carrying a plastic bag in hand. I was tempted to greet at least one of them and talk to him. A little further away I saw the Darwin Hotel Bar, there I saw a man in his forties heavily drunk, sitting on the steps of the bar. And another sight of two women in western dress heavily drunk swinging on the road and trying to cross the road.

The aborigines, the natives of Australia nearly for the past fifty thousand years inhabiting the Australian continent once independent, dignified people, though in a primitive state, have lost their dignity and self – respect. They were made economically dependent, culturally inferior and psychologically crippled with drinking. Some of them look sickly. Perhaps the only things common between the natives and the settlers are the English language and Christian faith. I am emotionally moved when I see the natives. They seem to be on the downward slope of degeneration – a ruined people.

**Friday, September 6, 1985**

In the forenoon on the invitation from the Department of Community Development of NT at Darwin gave a talk to officials at the department on Developing Entrepreneurship among the natives. They appreciated the approach I have suggested for development.

Ten minutes prior to my writing this (10.50 PM local time) the tooth that was shaky causing pain and inconvenience for more than 3 years came off. I worked on it for a few minutes and pulled it off and disposed it of in the waste paper basked in the room.

I thought of Visal. She often used to warn me, stop me from meddling with this tooth that left me today. Goodbye to the tooth. Its neighbor in the lower front row is likely to follow suit soon, since it is shaky and may leave me soon.

**Saturday, September 7, 1985**

Sri Padmanathan (from Sri Lanka, Settled in Australia) took me to the beach in the evening. My wish was to touch the waters of Pacific Ocean and sprinkle that water on my head. We had a stroll on the beach close to the waters. I saw for the first time in life Australian women with bare breasts tanning their bodies, stretching their bodies supine on the sands with a strip of cloth covering their genital, the only part they covered.

To me it was disgusting. Women here as scantily dressed, very casually dressed, their breasts, exposed save the nipples. They look more masculine and less of femininity, sexually not attractive. You find every second woman smoking. I do not understand where they are drifting to. They seem to be moving towards which may be called civilized savagery.

## SUNDAY, SEPTEMBER 8 1985

**Darwin–Denpasar–Jakarta**

Mr. Tony Wright was kind enough to drive me to the Darwin Airport. We were rather early to the airport. The reporting time was 12.15 PM. During his stay with me Tony told me some details about the development of Aborigines in Australia. He made some significant observations.

1. Some of the tribes are proud people and that sense of pride is a positive factor for development.
2. Their sense of justice, method of meeting justice is different. It is immediate, mostly physical punishment slashing or piercing a part of the body or killing the alleged offender or one who has caused harm, injustice to other.
3. The Aborigines were allowed to drink since 1960's.
4. When they drink they become aggressive.
5. Incidence of crime has increased in their case.
6. Social security payments to the Aborigines as in the case of whites has made them lazy.
7. The Australian white man's paternalistic approach to integrate them with the whites has misfired and the situation has become worse in the case of the Aborigines.

I thanked Tony, a friendly man. Back to Jakarta from Darwin via Denpasar changing flight at Denpasar and on 9th to Bandung.

**Wednesday, September 11, 1985**

I get emotionally touched when I listen to some Tamil and Telugu songs. I discovered a few days ago All India Radio Tamil Program for South-East Asia from 6.30 – 7.30 (Indonesia Thailand time). Last evening there were the old well known songs of Thyagaraja Bhagavathar.

Since time permits now while on such visits I keep in touch with B.B.C, Radio Australia, VOA, and All India Radio. I seldom listen to Moscow.

In the forenoon today got US $ 1000/- in the bank. Accompanied by Akmadi bought a medium sized Echoloc suit case, four batik shirts, a purse for Visal and T. Shirt for Baby.

**Saturday, September 14, 1985**

It is one month since I left Bangkok. Due to poor food, my own cooking without vegetables, I have lost weight and developed some itching all over my body. Dreaming and counting days to get back to Visal. She occupies my mind all through my waking moments.

**Monday, September 16, 1985**

Today is our 32nd marriage anniversary. We have completed 31 years of marriage characterized by several emotional upsurges, misunderstandings and with intense love for our endearing, beautiful five children. When I am away from the family my feelings go to the children and Visal, Bujja and Narasing.

I remember Mother and Father today. Mother is my spiritual guardian. The sage father to me is like Bhagawan Ramana Maharishi.

**Wednesday, September18, 1985**

Last night, I had terrifying pain causing perspiration and giddiness. I meddled with the other front tooth, neighbour to the one that came off in Darwin. I thought it too with a little shaking and a crude pull will come off. I pulled it badly. It did not. But it caused such a pain and for a few minutes, I felt dizzy and immediately collapsed on the bed and throughout the waking hours I did not meddle with or manoeuvre over it. I know I will be losing it soon. It will leave a gap in my mouth. I am worried about the clarity of my speech and my voice once I lose this shaky tooth. I think of Visal. She is more concerned about my teeth than myself.

**FRIDAY, SEPTEMBER 20 1985**

**Bandung**

Started reading "KGB – the Hidden Hand' by John Barron. The book deals with the ghastly activities perpetrated and carried out by the secret police KGB in Soviet Russia. The activities pictured in the book are horrifying, devilish, totally bereft of human element, a lunatic morbid behaviour of human machines engaged in those merciless, tortures and killings.

**Wednesday, October 2, 1985**

Mahatma Gandhiji's birthday. I was asked by the Indian Association at AIT (comprising Indian faculty, their families and the students altogether around 150 members) to give a talk on Gandhiji. The function was at the Korea House at 5 P.M. I spoke on Gandhiji for 19 minutes and I taped my talk. It was appreciated. The talk as recorded is as follows:

We remember Gandhiji as the Father of Indian Nation. But the entire mankind remembers Gandhiji as the inventor of "Satyagraha' as a peaceful agitator of Civil Disobedience and Non-Cooperation and as the man who has conceived the concept of Swadeshi. The idea of Civil Disobedience was conceived by David Henry Thoreau, a great friend of Ralph Waldo Emerson, the 19$^{th}$ century American philosopher, and a great intellectual, poet and writer. Thoreau was arrested for nonpayment of the poll tax. He protested against slavery and the Mexican war. Thoreau's confinement of one night gave birth to his essay on Civil Disobedience. His essay "Civil Disobedience" a classic of individualism (1849), inspired believers in passive resistance. He recorded his simple life on Walden Pond, Concord 1845-47 in Walden. Thoreau advised his countrymen to simplify their private lives and their government too for he was a supreme individualist. Leo Tolstoy received a copy of Civil Disobedience from Thoreau. Gandhiji, it is reported has received a copy of Thoreau's essay on Civil Disobedience and Non-Cooperation from Leo Tolstoy. Gandhiji and Tolstoy were in correspondence but they have not met personally.

Gandhiji as a human individual was a colossus and it is amazing how he combined in himself such sterling and unique facets of personality. We may here briefly mention a few facets of Gandhiji. Gandhiji as a barrister, as a shrewd politician, as a spiritual practitioner, as an able organizer, as a great leader and as an unfailing correspondent. There is no record of any complaint that Gandhiji has not answered the letters addressed to him by the young and the old from within the country and from all over the world. Today you are not sure of getting a reply to your letter addressed to a Prime Minister or a President. Further, Gandhiji was a great experimenter with truth. He was a scientist in spirit and temperament. He was a methodical worker, a great inventor of social technique of Satyagraha, a manager of time and people. Inspite of his busy schedule, he was a devoted husband. He was a strict parent and the general complaint about Gandhiji was that he was so much devoted to his children. Gandhiji as a friend was trustworthy. He was a journalist and a writer and believer in God, the man who preached what he practiced, the equality of Man. He was a man of simplicity. Gandhiji as man was tough as a diamond but at the same time he was affable and friendly. The people of India and Britain experienced him as tough as a diamond. We see in Gandhiji a blend of ancient traditions and modernity. Among the scientists he was a scientist, among the statesmen he was a statesman, among the farmers he was a farmer and among children he was a child. He had that kind of elasticity of personality. He can rise to the heights of Himalayas when an occasion arises and come down to the earth and be as simple as a farmer. Another amazing thing that we find in Gandhiji is the consistency of thought, talk and deed, what we call 'Thrikarana Suddhi'. Very often we think something, talk something and do things entirely different from our thoughts and talk. He advocated what he believed in and practiced. He did what he asked others to do. Most of the things that he preached and practiced were based on his experiments and only when he found efficacy and usefulness of things, he advocated such things to others. His great contribution is India's Independence and other than that in the context of growing aggression and violence, is his principle of non-violence. With the increasing competition and political and economic monopolistic tendencies, Gandhiji's principle of non-violence and the philosophy of 'Unto This Last' become more and more relevant and significant as the mankind moves into the future.

Gandhiji's greatness and simplicity and unbudging determination is reflected in the event of his invitation to meet George V, the King and Emperor during the Round Table Conference in 1930's. The Princes, Kings, Rajas and other Chiefs were invited on one condition that they should enter the Palace to meet the Emperor in a formal suit. This was prescribed to every invitee. But Gandhiji insisted that he would enter the Royal Palace and meet the Emperor in his typical simple loin cloth and Khadhi cloth covering his body. During this time Sir Samuel Hoare was the Secretary of State for India. He pleaded and persuaded Gandhiji to attend the Royal function in the prescribed attire. But

Gandhiji did not budge and insisted that if at all he were to meet the Emperor he will only meet him in his loin cloth. It was a situation where the Royal Protocol did not allow an invitee meeting the Emperor not in the prescribed dress and Gandhiji was such a force in India that he cannot be ignored and ultimately and reluctantly the British Royalty had to concede Gandhiji entering the Palace and meeting Gorge V in his loin cloth. That was the strength of his character.

Let us also look at the elasticity of the personality of Gandhiji. He had the felicity in conversing with eminent people and the ease and the simplicity with which he could talk to children and common people.

Further, when we think of the National Five Year Plans, Macro and Micro, the concept of planned rural development owes its genesis to Mahatma. During independence movement Gandhiji came up with an eighteen item Rural Reconstruction program. It was a comprehensive program addressing the multifarious rural development needs. We can imagine the vision that Gandhiji had the aspects that he covered in his rural reconstruction program.

We may briefly run through questions Gandhiji addressed in his rural reconstruction program. On the Economic front he emphasized on the protection and popularization of Khadi. He popularized Khadi and Charka, as symbol of village economy. He focused on the development of cattle. He touched upon the social front and fought for communal unity. He became a martyr in establishing communal harmony and unity. He fought for the removal of untouchability. Seldom we realize the black mark and stigma of untouchability. Gandhiji was the first man to enlighten the people and facilitate the entry of the Harijans into temples. He fought for prohibition and for equal status for women. Whether it was Sarojini Naidu or Kasturbha and other women associates with him in the freedom movement never found him discriminating women in any sphere.

We have around 500 Adivasi tribes in India who have not been until recent decades in the main stream of Indian politics and society. They were exploited by the plains people. Gandhiji in his constructive program focused on the ways of developing the Adivasis and integrating them into the main stream of Indian society.

On the educational front, we had the legacy of Mecaulay's education which was something alien not fitting with the Indian traditions and value system and conditions in the rural areas. He advocated the adoption of basic education. He thought of the bulk of the population in India being illiterate, he advocated Adult Education, Adult literacy in terms of reading, writing and arithmetic. Because of the advent of the English language, the regional languages had a setback and gradually receding to the minority status and using of English became a fashion. Gandhiji advocated the development of regional languages and adoption of Hidustani as a National lingua franca.

He focused on health. Some of you might have read his little book entitled "Key to Health". He practiced and advocated Naturopathy. He focused on improving village sanitation. He worked for eradication of leprosy and he personally dressed a leprosy associate who was a great Sanskrit Scholar.

On the political side, he strived for educating the farmers, peasants and the labor and to make them politically sensitive. He focused on the students and their involvement in the national affairs.

During his Shabermati and Sevagram days, Gandhiji personally participated in sanitary drives, sweeping the streets and cleaning the toilets. He advocated what is called Wardha type of trench latrines, wherein the night soil could be used as precious organic manure. He tried to popularize a fuel saving Maganchula (oven) in the village. We may here recall a story of Gandhiji's simplicity and his sense of dignity of labour. While he was at Sevagram in early 1930's some of the houses in the Sevagram village, the neighborhood to the Ashram, caught fire. Along with the villagers, the immates in the Ashram ran to extinguish the fire. These people have picked up an assortment of vessels and pots to carry water in order to extinguish the fire. He could find only broken tub and he filled it with water and went running to the place, carrying the tub on his shoulders. That was the sense of duty, simplicity and dignity of labout on the part of Gandhiji. This episode is recorded in Kaka Saheb Kalekar's book "Rare Glimpses of Bapuji".

Gandhiji has moulded and promoted thousands of leaders in India infusing in them patriotism and love for their motherland. Thousands of them followed him sacrificing their education and career. Gandhiji was a movement and a great era in the history of the World. Gandhiji was proud of India and we are proud of Gandhiji.

**Sunday, October 20, 1985**

Visal and the children joined a group of Sri Lankan students and visited Siam Park. I was happy to know that Baby has gone for the circular train, the long slide, the terrifying disco and several other bone-creaking play devices at the park. He is bold and adventurous. Jeji is a contrast to him like me.

In the night just before meal Visal flared up on my smoking, threatening that she would break the ash trays and burn the cigarette packs. She was wild.

**Friday, November 1, 1985**

The Thai, celebrate today their Loy Krothang which is similar to Karthika Deepam in south India. It is celebrated on the AIT campus, the faculty, students and the families of faculty participate in the function. Met Prof. Nishino (Vice –

President for Academic Affairs, AIT) in the function. I asked him about the status of religion in Japan. He said that their native religion was Shintoism. He added that some fifteen hundred years ago they took to Buddhism, but paradoxically the Dhammapada in Pali has not been translated into Japanese. The priests during the past centuries kept the knowledge of the text to themselves which gave them status and reverence while the common people had no access to the holy text and lacked that knowledge. Now the intellectual level of the people of Japan is very high while the priests are lower in knowledge in the fields of science and technology and the priests are no more held in high esteem by the people. Buddhism today matters only in observing the traditional customs in marriages and death ceremonies. Otherwise the religious observances are on the decline and in the days to come Prof. Nishino opined that Buddhism will wane in its importance and the Confucianism which has been there prior to the advent of Buddhism into Japan will become the faith of the Japaneese. I thanked Prof. Nishino for the time he spared in sharing with me the status of religion in Japan.

**Sunday, November 3, 1985**

In the evening had my first artificial teeth at the Rangsit Dental Clinic. Feel a bit uncomfortable with the denture in mouth. Better to be without teeth than with artificial ones.

**December 2 to 8, 1985**

Took Visal, Jeji and Baby along with me on a tour to Southern Thailand along with the students of HSD. It is arranged by the Division of Human Settlements (HSD). The group comprised forty including Nazrul and his family, Harvey Demaine and Detlef Kammier. The tour was well organized and we visited Phuket, Hat Yai, Songkla and Surathani. The places were interesting. What attracted me were the landscape, the hills, forests, luxurious vegetation and the highly developed towns and cities with adequate infrastructural facilities. One disgusting thing is the open prostitution among Thai women mostly patronized by the westerners. You can choose a fish, a shrimp and a woman without any inhibition or obstruction. It is highly permissive society. The children enjoyed the tour. My problem of course was food.

**Friday, December 13, 1985**

Attended the forty fifth graduation ceremony of AIT. Six of my advisees (Master Degree) have graduated today. Helal, Amin (Bangladesh), Pete, Mibs (The Philippines), Siddharata (India) and Daeng (Thailand). Prior to and after the graduation ceremonies some of my current advisees and former devisees requested me to join them for a photograph.

**Monday, December 16, 1985**

By 10.00 in the morning, unexpectedly I had a call from Prof. Nishino's secretary that the Professor wants to see me at his office. Until I reached his office I was anxious and nervous as to what should be the reason to call me. It turned out to be nomination as a resource person to a German GTZ – AIT conference on Technological Extension of Educational and Research Institutions. I agreed to be the resource person representing the Asian Institute of Technology. Prof. Nishino explained to me that normally, he as the Vice-president for Academic Affairs should be the resource person, alternately, Prof. Pama, the Vice-president for Development should be the resource person but he added that he was not sure that he would continue at AIT beyond August 1986 and that Pama was busy man and so a Senior Faculty like me is the right person to play that role. I thanked Prof. Nishino for the confidence he has in me.

**Thursday, December 26, 1985**

Visit to the Khao Yai National Park with a group of Tamil Sangam students mostly from Sri Lanka. Visal and Jeji were with me. The night halt was at some lodge at the Park. Visal volunteered to prepare Pulihora (Tamarind Rice) for all the people for the night. Luckily Visal and I were given a separate room, while others slept in the common half. In the night we went on a tour of the park on a highly raised truck. We could sight only three deer.

In the visit, my chief interest was the forest, the family of tress, some towering as aristocratic giants, some struggling as if in congested slums, all intent and struggling hard to survive. The society of trees, plants & grass is cosmopolitan one, different, but all having the same environment. It is a struggle and survival of the fittest. I like nature and want to be close to nature.

**Friday, December 27, 1985**

Visit to a water falls near the national park (Thailand). Lunch was a problem. Jeji took only a few pieces of papaya, I had some vegetable and papaya.

Out of ignorance, I spoiled 12 units of the film roll.

Since it is a protected area, no plant species is allowed to be taken out. Mrs. Sadhanada found some curry leaf plants and plucked some. But this was watched by the guards there, and while we were on the bus, just before leaving that point, three fellows got into the bus, and took away the plants that were with Sadhanada's. we had four plants managed by Visal. I was keeping them hidden on my side. I did not return the plants. On reaching the dorm to collect our baggage, hid the plants in a wet towel and stuffed it in a hard bag. Until we passed the check point, I was worried and apprehensive possible check while leaving the park. But to our relief, there was no check.

On reaching home (5.20 PM) prepared a pot and Visal and I Planted the four plants, two tiny, one medium and one big relatively speaking. We would be very happy if they survived.

In the visit, my interest was the forest, the family of trees, some towering as aristocratic giants, some struggling as if in congested slums, all intent and struggling hard to survive. The society of trees, plants, grass is a cosmopolitan one : different, but all having the same environment. It is a struggle and survival of the fittest.

I like nature and want to be close to nature.

**Saturday, January 5, 1986**

Left Jakarta by train to Bandung, it was an easy journey. On the train Hiran told me of him and his family, especially of his father, his innovative ideas and poor management of his projects. Hiran was the first Asian to secure a first class in his maters at Cambridge and he was forty when he became the Vice-Chancellor of Colombo University.

**Friday, January 10, 1986**

In order to pre-test the questionnaire, Hiran and I visited a village called Mynaeti, 20 Km from Subhang. I was more interested in observing the village life. The behaviour and the hospitality extended to us by the village headman is similar to that of a Panchayat President in Andhra Pradesh. The women with just bras (though Muslim) move about freely. Another beauty of the village is it is situated amidst thick vegetation.

There is an interesting and innovative practice of calls of nature on the part of these villagers. Both the sexes answer calls of nature squatting on an elevated, cubical of bamboo structure about 6 feet high put up in open fields with knee-deep water. The enclosure is scanty and there is barely any privacy. They say it is organic fertilizing and it is direct application of human excreta as manure to the fields. Once, a particular field is covered, they shift the improvised bamboo structure to another field which is also flooded and usually close to the village. The matter (excreta) is dissolved in the water and thus foul stink is prevented. This practice is said to be quite common in all the villages on Java Island.

**Friday, January 24, 1986**

Visit to Cikadu. The participants have arranged a meeting with the youth of the village. I was asked to address them, but I did not want to give any lecture to the villagers and in turn I asked them to raise questions if any. One young man asked me whether Indonesian films are shown in India. I told him, none. And in return several people voiced that they watch Indian Hindi movies here. Further, they asked me questions on Raj Kapoor and Amitabh Bachchan. On their wish, Hiran and I had to shake hand in the Indonesian fashion with some 60 men and women who stood and moved in a file.

**Wednesday, January 29, 1986**

Shocked over U.S. Challenger's tragedy in which seven astronauts were killed.

Today, on my visit to Bandung Institute of Technology, I was surprised to see Ganesha as the symbol/emblem of BIT, unusual and unimaginable to find Muslims using a Hindu God as their symbol. Without my raising any question when I was gazing the idol of Ganesh with an expression of amazement in my face, one member of the BIT told me that Ganesha symbolizes wisdom and science. Another man who accompanied me from the LIPI office asked me, "Do you know of Ganesha?". For a while I kept silent and then answered him that Ganesha comes from India.

## TUESDAY, FEBRUARY 4 1986

**Bandugn**

**A Terrifiying Encounter**

Five minutes to twelve midnight when I was half asleep, I heard the buzzer sound in my room, I was jostled to wakeup and immediately could not figure out who pressed the buzzer at that hour. It is Sankuriang Hotel, where I have been staying for the past one month and in the same room where I stayed for a month last year also. The buzzer chirped again. I was startled and felt uneasy and nervous. I shouted, who it was. No response from the caller. I just pulled the window curtain and saw a figure standing outside the room. It could not be the room boy I thought within myself nor it could be Prof. Hiran Dias, who was staying in another room on the same floor, and that he won't press the buzzer. Frightened, I switched on the light in the room and pushed aside the curtain and saw a young, well dressed and groomed beautiful woman standing outside close to the window. I went dry and in a nervous tone asked her with gestures why she came and what she wanted. She put on a smile and with all steadiness gestured pointing to her wrist indicating as a query what time it was. I did not open the door. I signaled to her to go away and I pulled back the curtain. She coolly walked away.

Doubtless, she was a call girl. She took a chance and knocked at my door. I assume that she should have entered the hotel at that odd hour only with the connivance of the security man at the gate and reception. I was so scared that I could not sleep until 2.00 AM.

**Sunday, February 16, 1986**

Visit to Athimanjeripet for the tonsure and ear-piercing ceremony of Tiny. This village is the birth place of mother. Her parents' house is in ruins. Of all the mother's, sisters and bothers, only two of mothers children, my brother and I have received university education and gained some professional position. Mother was born and brought up in this village. Today, we have very little contact with the descendants of her natal family.

Around 11.30 AM, we went to the Muniswara Shrine to carry out the tonsure and ear-piercing for Tiny in a small procession, Pandu carrying on his head a basket containing the articles for propitiating the deity. But what made me sad was the animal sacrifice customarily associated with this particular deity. In a sense, it is a meat eating deity. It is not actual eating, but acceptance on the part of the deity. For Tiny's tonsure, a black goat, a cock and miserable looking pigling were the victims of sacrifice. I objected to killing of these animals but the group prevailed on me and the force of practice was mightier and it prevailed.

Tiny shone like a tiny star and dazzled as a beautiful doll. After tonsure Tiny looked another beauty.

**Sunday, March 16, 1986**

Disillusioned over the violence in several parts of the world. It looks as though the world is leading to catastrophe. The only thing that is serious is knowledge of self and closing the eyes with no desire.

**Friday, March 21, 1986**

Last night, I listened to the recordings of the village people. Emotionally I was transported to the village and felt happy. This afternoon I played the voice of sweet TINY. For some days now, since I returned from home, I was not able to locate the particular cassette where in TINY's voice, his rhymes were recorded, I thought I have misplaced or that it was lost. But I found it this afternoon.

**Tuesday, April 1, 1986**

Often I get a feeling that I remain the old, normal, not so intelligent and a simple man of the village and not the man known to others as Setty, as a Faculty at the Asian Institute of Technology, a Father of five beautiful children and a grandfather now. It appears that Setty to me is different from Setty to others. A feeling of stranger to myself.

**Tuesday, April 8, 1986**

I felt rather elated to receive a copy of Laghu Udyog Samachar, a publication of the Department of Small-Scale

Industries, Government of India, New Delhi, wherein my article on "Role of Banks in Entrepreneurship Development" appears – October 1985 issue. The Editor J.C. Jain writes in his covering letter that the article 'Has evoked considerable interest and was widely appreciated'.

**Thursday, May 1, 1986**

Field visit to some projects in the Chieng mai and Chieng Rai area in the north of Thailand. The group consisted of nine participants from Indonesia, two research assistants and myself as the program co-ordinator. I took Visal with me. It was a long journey over 700 KM on an A/c mini bus. It was an overnight journey from Bangkok. Reached, Chieng Mai by 8.00 in the morning and checked-in at Prince Hotel. Immediately left for Mesa Watershed project.

**Friday, May 2, 1986**

Visit to Doi Intanon Kings project where they work with some hill tribes. It is reported that these hill tribes earlier were engaged in growing narcotic herbs and in order to dissuade them from this practice and as a remunerative substitute the tribes are motivated and assisted in growing different kinds of flowers. Since it is the King's project, it has all the special attention.

The variety of flowers grown here is quite exciting – the nature as a master and man co-operating with nature. One has to see and enjoy the wonderful world of flowers of diverse colours and size. Cultivating these flower plants on the slopes of hills and in the hilly terrain appears to be a tough job. On one hand there is scarcity of land, tribes are emotionally attached to the hills and difficult to move them to plains. Most of them are from Burna and Laos. It is a sensitive area.

**Thursday, June 19, 1986**

Spoke to Dr Yogesh Atal on telephone. On my request,

he agreed to contribute a foreword to the 1st volume of the Valayar study. Hope things would assume shape.

**Monday, July 28, 1986**

Letters (all in one envelope) from Jeji, Baby, Babu and Kutta, all wishing a happy birthday to their mother. What touched me in Babu's letter was asking me the full quotation from Oliver Goldsmit's "A City Night Piece:

"Let me no longer waste the night over the pages of antiquity nor the sallies of contemporary genius but pursue the solitary walk".

I often remember these lines. These lines of Goldsmith touch me, I become emotional to the point of shedding tears.

**Thursday, July 31, 1986**

A letter from Prof. K.N. Sahay (my advisor for Ph.D., Ranchi University, Department of Anthropology). He writes that Prof. L.P. Vidyarthi (Chairman of the Department of Anthropology), overworked to his death against the advice of doctors and his death has created a vacuum". Prof. Vidyarthi was responsible for my Ph.D. registration with Ranchi University. A great scholar, who was the second president from Asia of the World Congress of Anthropology and Ethnology (1973-78).

**Saturday, August 2, 1986**

Adiga, one of my students from Nepal, originally from Udipi, South India gave me a brief account of Pasupathi Temple in Nepal, the practice of South Indian Brahmin, only to serve as priests at the Pasupathi temple that is the priests to be at the temple should have born in South-India. He clarified to me that Ghurkas are not an ethnic group, but all people who hail from this district called Gurkha. Traditionally, people from this district joined army and some Gurkhas are still in the British army. Adiga also told me how the monarchy functions in Nepal, a feudalistic society.

**Sunday, August 3, 1986**

Visal's 48th birthday. Till 3 PM, she was busy preparing food, some extra items to observe her birthday.

She as usual was in her new sari and with gold chain with newly bought pathakam. She likes jewels and also likes to display them.

At 6.30, there was a surprise visit of K.L. Bhat, his wife, his young daughter and one NR. Appa Rao and his wife. Mr. Rao is the Managing Director of a company, they had some vada, Payasam etc.

I had a different picture of Bhat on seeing him. I had to revise my image. He looks a man of action.

Rao is in his late sixties, (he looks so). He showed interest in anthropology, on learning of my Anthropological background. He said that Thai culture is older to Indian and Egyptian civilization. I listened to him and was not in a position to contradict his statement.

Visal looks happy. She remembered the children.

**Thursday, August 7, 1986**

A sad letter from Krishna that his mother Ademma died on 28.07.1986 and the last ceremony was today (07.08.1986).

I do not know whether I should call it some premonition. When I left home after lunch at 2 PM, Visal was angry that I was leaving for the division and I should have stayed at the house for some more time and helped her, a thought came to me that there should be a letter today of somebody's demise.

I had intimate relation with Ademma, though disgusting, she was affectionate, people oriented she had good and bad days. The last couple of years were hard economically and in terms of her health.

I visited her along with Visal last February. She was ill, immobilized with some internal problem. I knew that I was seeing her for the last time.

The relation between Ademma and her husband Bangaru was illustrious. He was simple, honest and innocent. He looks now a legendary figure, a character in Mahabharata.

I pray for the soul of Ademma.

## THURSDAY, AUGUST 21 1986

### AIT

I have a tendency to shy away from formal functions and some reluctance to formal and gaudy dress. But at the same time, this kind of posture and behaviour leaves me with a feeling that I should have been there and I should have had that kind of dress, but I did not. I am more toward simplicity and informality. When I look at myself from the angle of worldly knowledge I am very marginal, with some little bits and scraps of knowledge while the whole body of knowledge of nature – physical chemical and biological is a mystery to me.

I like to compare the ethnic/national groups on the AIT campus to a zoo, wherein you have different species of animals, but with no interaction and contact amongst them. Each nationality considers that it is superior to others, by skin, by wealth, by language and by geographical location.

There was the 47th graduation function today. I did not attend the function, since the administration expects all faculty in formal dress.

### Friday, December 12, 1986

(From December 11 – 20 I am on official mission visiting some of the institutes in South India for academic collaboration with AIT – Human Settlements Development

Division and From December 21 – January 6, 1987 on home leave).

As part of this mission visited the National Institute of Rural Development (NIRD) Hyderabad. Met Dr. Muthiah, who is in-charge of my visit. Met Mr. Lyngdoh, IAS, Deputy Director General of NIRD and briefed him about the collaboration AIT is seeking with NIRD.

In the afternoon, I gave a seminar for two hours (3-5PM) on "People's Participation in Rural Development". The seminar was attended by some 50 persons : Directors, Deputy Directors, Assistant Directors and the other staff of the Institute. I spoke on the subject of one and a half hours and answered questions from the audience for 30 minutes. The seminar went on well.

A little reflection on my visit to NIRD. Here is an Institute to which I have applied for a Research Associate post 20 years ago, but today with all modesty I may say that I am looked upon as an important visitor to the Institute where you had top officials as your audience. Incidentally, Dr. Muthiah, present in-charge DG of NIRD, was on the selection committee when I was selected for a faculty position at the SIET Institute, Hyderabad way back in 1974. I felt overwhelmed.

**Monday, December 15, 1986**

Madras to Madurai by Air. At the Madurai Airport Mrs. R.S., (Godavari), Boraian, Rajaram's father and brother were waiting to receive me. I could not at first look, recognize Mrs. R.S. She looked old, pale and I told her that she should not have come to the Airport to receive me. Boraian, who was my student has grown tall, him too I could not recognize until he mentioned his name.

To Madurai city, lunch in a restaurant hosted by Mrs. R.S. At the restaurant Mrs. R.S. introduced me to a visiting faculty at Gandhigram Rural Institute from Grambling State

University, USA. I was happy to learn form her that she got a photostat copy of my article on People's Participation in Rural Development from the Madurai School of social work.

Reached Gandhigram around 3.30 PM. My visit now to GRI is after 12 years. I could see many changes here during this period. Met Prof. R. Subramanian (R.S.), Soraja, the stenographer, Vekataraman (her husband), Prof. Joseph, my old English professor, Prof. M.G. Gopala Krishnan, Dr. Radha Krishna, Prof. Warrier, Tamil Prof. Rengarajan, Prof. Selvaraj, Porf. V. Krishnamurthy, Prof. Chellappa and several others. It was akin to home coming because I spent around 12 years at Gandhigram Rural Institute as a student and as a faculty.

In the evening, visited Valayapatti, dearest to me, the nuclear village for my doctoral thesis on the Valayar of South India. Some of my respondents have passed away; Thammanamabalam, Pachainambalam, Dandi and some others. Faces of others I met have changed. Infants 12 years ago at the time of my field work who don't know me are pre-adolescents. I felt happy to meet and talk to my friends some of the chief informants of my study who were available at the village during my visit : Chembagam, Palanichamy, Chemban, Madayanai and several others. I was touched by their affection. It was an emotional meeting for me. Gave Rs. 300/- to Palanichamy towards the celebration of their deities. Took leave of them – an enduring and friendly community.

**Tuesday, December 16, 1986**

In the afternoon had a meeting with Mr. Devendra Kumar, Vice-Chancellor of Gandhigram Rural Institute. Discussed with him the possible kind of collaboration between GRI and HSD of AIT. The V.C., a Gandhian, a close associate of Vinobha Bhava is said to be an authority on technology for rural development. Met Mrs. Devendra Kumar who happens to be the sister of shipping magnet Jayanthi Teja, a Telugu.

**Wednesday, December 17, 1986**

In the morning met Mrs. Devendra Kumar, who happens to be a Telugu, the sister of Jayanthi Teja, the shipping magnate. Took leave of her and her VC husband and of RS and Mrs. Rs.

Boraian took me to his home at Chinnalapatti, on our way to the Madurai airport. On the information given by Marugan in Madras that Karuppannan was SI at Sholavandan, went there and found that he was not there. I requested the S.P there to contact others through wire, where Karuppannan was said to be working. He could not contact.

**Thursday, December 18, 1986**

As part of the mission, Visited the Asian Institute of Rural Development, Bangalore. The Director, Rajashekar was away during my visit and met Dr. Hundli a retired man incharge of training. He was waiting for me. He took me to the Institute's Training Centre located in the outskirts of the city. They were running a training program on land policy for 20 Asian participants. I was requested to speak to the participants on Rural Development. My Session lasted for one and a half hour.

My next visit to Institute for Social and Economic Change (ISEC). Met the Director Dr. Thimmaiah and gave a seminar at the institute for two hours on People's Participation in Rural Development. The audience comprised some forty ISEC's faculty. Discussed with Dr. Thimmaiah and his senior colleagues the aspects of collaboration between ISEC and AIT. Dr. Thimmaiah was kind enough to drop me at Hotel Chalukya. While Visal and I were at the hotel, Guna and Suresh came with a telegram sent by brother from the village addressed to N.R.C. (N. Radhakrishna Chetty) asking him to inform me that I should immediately proceed to village. It was 10.30 PM. when I had the message that Narasing was serious.

**Friday, December 19, 1986**

Took the morning 7.30 bus to Chittoor. On the way while on the bus Visal asked me (as she did often) the amount of money I have sent to sister. I did not answer her. I evaded the question. She got her characteristic tantrums and at the Kolar stopover she got down from the bus and wanted to get back to Bangalore. I pleaded with her but it was of no avail and I had to physically drag her into the bus. A terrible an awful experience with her.

At Chittoor took a taxi to the village. Narasing is just a skeleton, very weak, does not take any food, he spoke to me a few words. My heart burnt, I was seeing him in his last days. Brother was here already since a few days attending on him. A few days ago Narasing was taken to CMC, Vellore and it was diagnosed blood cancer.

**Tuesday, December 23, 1986**

Arranged a taxi and took Narasing to CMC hospital. Visal, Kannamma (Narasing's wife), Rama Murthy and I were with Narasing. The doctors examined him and told us that there was no hope. I told him that the doctors said that there was no need and he could take the prescribed medicine at home. I lied to him. He did not know what disease he was suffering from. (P.S. : He died without knowing it). We got him back to the village.

**Thursday, December 25, 1986**

With a heavy heart I took leave of my dearest brother Narasing, kissed his beautiful hands. I like his palms and fingers. He partly sat up in his bed and told me, "Anna, be courageous, don't worry and afraid of, go peacefully". These were his last words to me. I really wanted to stay in the village, but Visal insisted that we should get back to Bangalore. Took leave of brother and sister and in the evening retuned to Bangalore.

## SUNDAY, DECEMBER 28 1986

**Bangalore**

The saddest Sunday. Around 9.00 in the morning Guna came to the hotel with the message that Narasing passed away this morning. The message was over telephone from Vellore given by Ramamurthy to one Thangavelu and from him to K. Purushotham and from Purushotham to his father-in-law N.R.C. Though Narasing's end was expected it shocked me. Dear Narasing is no more. As I gathered later in the village Narasing was quite conscious until 5.00 in the morning today. At 5.00 he called Sriramulu (his younger son) to help him walk upto the bathroom close to the hall to answer calls of nature. After he did it, he had the wash with hot water and while returning to the room he put down his head and called 'Sriramulu' and in a matter of 5 minutes he breathed his last. It was 5.15 AM.

Narasing, during his childhood, teens, and until his marriage has his normal health trouble – free life. During the past 20 years he had a miserable life both in Bangalore and at the village. He was a kind of loner, highly intelligent, witty and humorous. He has indulged in alcohol and that took him away. The only thing I refused to give him was a cigarette when he was on his death bed on 23rd or so. When I went to see him, he signaled to me in his usual way for a puff. I told him that smoking in that state my result in some complication and so did not give him cigarette. He kept silent. I felt for his urge but did not comply with his last request to me.

Narasing was a philosopher, a loving person. I pray for his soul.

Narasing's body was buried close to mother's in the 'Vanka' (Rivulet near the village). The last look I had of him before the body was covered in the grave is still suffocating me. I felt that I was being buried. His physical journey ended today. He remains in my heart. I pray of his soul.

Brother writes "Narasing had no ambition in life. He had no ill-will towards anybody. He never interfered with anybody. He had no attachment to his wife and children. He underwent many difficulties. All of them were his own making. May his soul rest in peace".

**Monday, December 29, 1986**

By 10.00 in the morning, Narasing's body was buried close to mother's in the 'Vanka' (rivulet near the village). The last look I had of him before the body was covered in the grave is still suffocating me. I felt that I was being buried. His physical journey ended today. He remains in my heart. I pray for his soul.

**Tuesday, February 10, 1987**

In his letter, brother writes to me (to AIT, Bangkok) that the last rites for Narasing was largely attended by our relatives. Of Narasing he writes :

"Narasing had no ambition in life. He had no ill-will towards anybody. He never interfered with anybody. He had no attachment to his wife and children. He underwent many difficulties. All of them were his own making. May his soul rest in peace".

The above feelings of brother aptly describe Narasing. Yes, Narasing was a sage-like man. Externally he looked miserable, but within a detached person.

**Monday, February 23, 1987**

A letter from brother speaking of his feelings about Narasing. He writes that the last day Narasing cooked food for himself and Bujja was December 5, 1986, 23 days before he passed away. Narasing has asked brother for a coffee filter, which brother purchased for him later and dear Narasing has no chance to use it. A sage has passed away.

**Saturday, April 11, 1987**

Gave a one hour lecture at Dhaka University, Department of Geography. The audience composed some faculty and sstudents.

**Sunday, June 21, 1987**

Today, I had an opportunity of seeing Mr. Jimmy Carter, former President of USA, during his visit to AIT.

I have been a regular listener of 'Letter from America from Alistair Cook over BBC. Today I listened to phone-in program wherein Cook answered questions. As I imagined, he first types out his letter from America, broadcast over BBC over the week-end and then speaks to the tape and the tape is flown to London. His is a sweet voice and he is supremely informed of events and people.

**Thursday, July 9, 1987**

In the night, on my request an Indian student Potey read my palm and asked me whether I had specific questions to ask him. To my questions he answered that I will get extension of contract, but getting promotion is doubtful and I may get some benefit before my sixtieth birthday and that he will not tell me the span of life, but death will be sudden. The latter part sent shudders into my body. For a while I felt giddy.

God is the only answer.

**Wednesday, July 15, 1987**

Watched a 'movie last night, entitled "Escape from Sabibor, the Nazi German Concentration Camp". It was horrible how the Jews were treated and enmasse killed in the concentration camps. The movie is based on real events that 300 out of 600 prisoners escapee from the concentration camp. How does Christianity go with the Germans?

**Tuesday, July 21, 1987**

His majesty, the king of Thailand visited AIT today. I was caught up more and concerned rather feeling uneasy about my wearing a tie and suit for this occasion. Prof. Venkatachalam helped me putting a knot to the tie and with that my ordeal was over.

H.M. The King spent around five hours on the campus. The King in Thailand, the longest reigning monarch in the world is revered and worshipped by the Thai people. In Thailand, the timings of radio and T.V. programs are flexible, whenever there were any royal visits and functions, the whole system operates on personal principles.

It was to observe the oddity in the case of those who had to appear in suits today – an expression of uneasiness and uncomfortableness in their faces. Myself also reflected in this.

**Saturday, August 1, 1997**

It respect to the values and religious beliefs and practices I do not find any difference between earlier centuries, middle ages and the present times. Maddening sectarianism especially among the Muslims and Christians – Sunny and Shiites, Catholic and Protestant killing each other, especially in the case of Muslims, a faith of extreme emotionalism and fundamentalism leaving no room for individual religious freedom. Religion should be an emancipator and should not enslave people to narrow corridors instigating people annihilate one another.

**Friday, August 14, 1987**

The major worldly things that make me anxious are the Valayar study publication and Jeji's marriage. The prediction speaks of rewards in August but none so far. May be end of this month.

Remembered Pandu, Visal, Jeji, Babu, Baby, Kutta and Tiny. God bless them.

Went to sleep at 12.30 AM.

**Saturday, August 15, 1987**

Inextricably a mixed day. Birth and death of two children in the family. Though Rajeevi died an 14th, he was cremated on 15th (1982). A tragedy in our family. So long, we and our children live the horrible life of Rajeevi will be remembered. I pray for his soul.

**Thursday, August 27, 1987**

I have a Japanese Citizen watch, but my problem is, I do not know how to set the digital timing. I am zero, when it comes to any skill related to gadgets and machines. I am out of tune with the present times.

**Friday, September 4, 1987**

Around 1.45 AM last night, I felt suffocation suddenly, hard to breathe and heavy coughing, hard to describe. I sat up on the bed perspiring and I thought that I may die. Felt uneasy and giddy. Rushing thoughts over Visal and the children and once I die this night, Visal would find my body on Tuesday when she arrives to Bangkok from Hyderabad. Terrific feeling. Prayed to Ramana to give me some more years of life and to die on the lap of Visal. I do not know the cause for the sudden happening.

**Saturday, September 5, 1987**

In the morning washed and cleaned up the pictures of deities and the puja articles used by Visal. In a way it was my intense thoughts of Visal.

Today my condition grew worse. I could not eat in the afternoon. Forced a little rice and dhal. By evening I felt miserable with the thought whether I will not see Visal at all.

I met Sunil's wife who is a medical doctor at their residence. She checked B.P. it was normal 135/85. gave some tablets for flatulence.

Stopped smoking.

Did not eat anything, on request Helal and Murthy slept at the house. I gave Helal telephone No. to reach Visal and Babu in any tragic event.

Very weak physically and mentally.

**Monday, September 7, 1987**

Feel very weak. Insensible urge to smoke a habit of nearly 45 years. In the morning two Guptas SP and CP came to see me. Prof. Venkatachalam returned from Malaysia.

Still slight pain on the left side. I strongly wish to see Babu, he was infinite love for me and all children too.

Thoughts over Visal that they should have left for Calcutta this evening.

My difficultly will be in managing two courses, especially filling usefully the lab hours.

Salutations to Ramana.

**Tuesday, October 27, 1987**

I am sixty today. I owe my existence to Brahman. Salutations to Para Brahman. Visal and I offered puja and she wished me a happy birthday and as a present she put around my neck a gold chain. I wore a safari suit for the first time in my life.

In the morning class today, a student asked me whether there was any occasion today of my having Kumkum Bottu (vermilion mark) on my forehead and new dress. I told her that today was my birthday. A few students who heard it shouted happy birthday.

After my class (9.40 AM) the 19 students in the class celebrated my birthday with cakes and candles. They asked me to blow off the lighted candles and they in a chorus sang happy birthday to you. It was in the classroom. It was overwhelming and it touched me. I thanked the students heartily.

**Saturday, November 8, 1987**

Visit to Taipei, Capital of Taiwan, Republic of China as a delegate to a conference organized by the International Association for Community Development, Brussels, Belgium.

Visal and Helal, (my student from Bangladesh) accompanied me upto Don Maung Airport. On way to Taipei, has a stopover for 40 minutes at Hong Kong Airport. Just has a glimpse of Hong Kong Port, highrise buildings and the hills. At Taipei airport two airport two young men received me and my stay was at Hero House Hotel. I was surprised to find that my roommate was Prof. Panwalkar of the Tata Institute of Social Science, Bombay. He is an old friend of mine.

**Tuesday, November 17, 1987**

Went on sight seeing through a tourist agency. One impressive scenery we visited was a four hundred million year old huge lime rock with deep and extensive caves. I took some photographs of the caves and the idols and shrines in the caves. I must mention here the disappointment we met with. The camera with full length of film was borrowed earlier by Shiva Shankar at AIT and when he returned it to us on 15$^{th}$ on the eve of our departure to Kuala Lumpur, I was under the impression that Shiva Shankar had loaded the camera with a new roll, since he has used our film. While taking the snaps, the camera was showing successive numbers of frames and I thought that film roll was inside, but when I pressed the rewinding knob it did not work.

Changed the batteries and yet no noise related to rewinding. Opened the camera and found that it was empty. Shiva Shankar failed to tell us that he had not loaded the camera with a film roll. We were disappointed since, we were left without the images of the primordial caves.

**Sunday, February 14 ,1988**

Visal and I received Prof. Devendra Kumar on his arrival at the Bangkok airport. He stayed with us and had dinner with us. In the course of discussion, sharing his ideas on Rural Development Technology, he gave apt and significant example of a creeper and how, the man who planted the seed shifted the support before the creeper could reach the support.

Prof. Devendra Kumar is a staunch believer and practitioner of Gandhian approach to development. He is a slow talking and highly confident man. He has positive approach to things and he is a real constructive worker.

**Sunday, February 21, 1988**

Sometimes, Visal reminds me of my weaknesses and provides me the spiritual guidance without knowing that she was doing so. She has faith in deities, but has an extreme degree of hatred especially toward brother, sister and Yasoda. May be in the case of brother and Yasoda, she has a reason to be so, but in the case of sister, it is unjustified.

**Friday, February 26, 1988**

Rather I was late in reaching Dr. S. Radhakrishan's English translation of Bhagavad Gita. Went through the lengthy Introduction which runs around 90 pages. I find answers to some of the doubts I had for a long time. Dr. Radhakrishnan is a giant in thought and language, a towering scholar in the Indian philosophy and the Hindu view of life.

**Wednesday, April 13, 1988**

In the afternoon Dr. Y.S. Rao, his mother and wife and Amisha and her tow daughters lunched with us. It was pleasure to speak to Dr. Rao, knowledgeable and spiritual man.

**Monday, June 13, 1988**

One piece of sadness is that Ramanujam (son of Pedda Geekam) died of heart failure a few months ago. He was a talented man, although he had little formal education. The saddening thing is that I have not met him for nearly 25 years.

Some eight years ago he spoke to me over/telephone in Hyderabad.

May his soul rest in peace.

**Tuesday, July 12, 1988**

By 7.00 AM we reached Gandhigram. Prof. R.S. was waiting for us at the campus gate with the vehicle. Immediately on reaching the guest house the Vice-Chancellor Prof. Devendra Kumar received us and we had breakfast and lunch with him at his residence. On the campus met my old colleagues : P.K. Kodandapani (in his case after 14 years), Dr. Subramanayam, Dr. Karthikeyan, Dr. Janakiraman, Dr. Surya (my old student), Prof. Narayana Swamy (my old student) and several others at the Institute.

The V.C. has arranged a meeting of the Heads of Departments and Deans and everyone was asked to speak about his activities. I addressed the group briefly mainly briefing them on AIT. Seated on the right side of the VC, I had a peculiar feeling of the importance given me.

Around ten in the night met my former English teacher Prof. M.G. Gopala Krishnan. Now he is retired from GRI and when I met him, the packing of household articles was in progress. He is an admirable teacher. With inimitable humour, an authority on English grammar and he is leaving for his home town in Kerala. Took leave of him. I can never forget the way he taught us Thomas Hardy's 'Far from the Madding Crowd and the Trial and Death of Socrates'.

**Saturday, July 30, 1988**

Reading through 'Talks with Sri Ramana Maharshi', I must say that I am fortunate that I came in touch with Ramana, my Guru.

**Monday, August 8, 1988**

It has been in long wish to purchase a two-in-one tape recorder and give it to brother with the tapes of my recitation of the entire Bhagavad Gita. Purchased one Sony tape recorder, three saris for Yasoda and shirts for brother and the children. I did this today with an intention that I could hand them over to brother when I visit Hyderabad and other places along with Dr. Paul Babarik on our research work next week.

**Friday, August 12, 1988**

At 4.30 PM. (I was alone at AIT) I played a few chapters of Bhagavad Gita on the tape-recorder I purchased for brother. I mused within myself that brother would listen to my voice and derive mental peace from the Gita.

At 5 PM. I went to see on the campus whether there was any telex message from Dr. Gnana Kannan of Administrative Staff College of India, Hyderabad about accommodation. There was one from him with 'No response'. Then I went down the scroll of telexes and I was shocked to see the telex form K. Purushotham, Hyderabad that brother passed away at 2 AM today and the cremation will take place tomorrow.

Immediately I tried to contact Bangalore over telephone to reach children or Visal, despite several attempts did not get the line. Later at 8 PM called Chowdhappa's (Bangalore) and requested his son Ashwin to send a cable to Bhasker (brother's son) Hyderabad that I could not reach Hyderabad from Bangkok tomorrow and that they may go ahead with the cremation. Later called Bangalore and informed the children of the sad demise of their uncle.

Brother was a Sage – Philosopher. He has suffered a great deal, monetary and domestic and of late, I suspect he has been under stress. He loved me a great deal. I saw him last month on 13th, a month ago, and his soul left his body. I pray for his soul.

**Saturday, August 13, 1988**

When brother passed away yesterday, he should have been 64 or 65. eldest of four of us – three brothers and a sister. He had smooth schooling upto SSLC (1944). He did work for one year and a few months in the Electricity Department in Bangalore. Later he joined Voorhis College in Vellore and left it after a few months and then he joined Sri Venkateswara College, Tirupathi (1946-48) for Intermediate and Pachaiyappa's College, Madras in 1948 for his B.Com, but could not complete some papers in Commerce and later in Hyderabad he secured a B.A. attending an evening college.

He married Yasoda on June 7, 1951 and the first son Rejeevi born on April 16, 1951 and the first son died on August 13, 1982 and cremated on August 15. Brother bore other four sons : Bhaskar, Murali, Suresh and Satish.

He joined the office of the Inspector General of Police, Madras as a clerk in 1950 through the service commission and retired in 1986 as a gazetted P.A. to DG of Police, Hyderabad.

In the office of the DG, he was known as a fine and conscientious government employee, with clean hands throughout his service.

He was calm, disciplined and philosopher – like man. He loved me greatly and was proud of my academic and career achievement. In terms of money, he suffered a great deal and in later years, a bit better. In our childhood, I do not remember to have played with him nor, did I have any close relationship with him as a child. Whereas Narasing and I were close as friends. I love brother. Since Rajeevi's tragic end by suicide, the relation between Visal and Yasoda and the children on both sides was strained. After six years or so, I visited bother's house in Hyderabad (July 13, 1988). It is my misfortune that I was in Bangkok when brother was cremated. I pray for the soul of my brother.

**Wednesday, November 2, 1988**

Thoughts over my two brothers, both of them suffered a great deal. Their affection for me was great. May their souls rest in peace?

**Friday, November 14, 1988**

Received five copies of the book on 'Small and Cottage Industries in Bangladesh' co-authored by Helal and me. It is based on research conducted in Bangladesh. Sent a copy to President Alistair North and Vice-President Prof. Eggers.

**December 25, 1988**

For some years now, I have been dreaming of visiting Ramanasramam at Thiruvrannamalai on December 25, left for Thiruvannamalai in the early hours with Visal and Baby. Visal was insistent on visiting Madurai and Gandhigram after Thiruvannamalai. I reluctantly agreed to it.

We reached the Ramanasramam by 10 AM. There was a considerable gathering of Indians and westerners and the abhishekam was in progress. To my pleasant surprise it was Ramana's birth anniversary, $109^{th}$ or $110^{th}$. Sat in the prayer hall for two hours, where Ramana's Samadhi lies and adjacent to it is his mother's, which is a temple now.

Bought Upadesa Saram of Ramana and his teachings. 'BE AS YOU ARE' edited by David Godman.

**Thursday, March 2, 1989**

Prof. Yogesh Atal called me in the morning to enquire whether his foreword has reached me. He came up with a suggestion that both of us join for writing three or four books on cross ethnic study of ritual and ceremonies associated with birth, initiation, marriage, death (of several caste groups in India) along the lines of my Valayar study. It is a good proposition and I agreed to the idea and told him that we shall try. Prof. Atal was on the phone for nearly 30 minutes.

**Monday, April 24, 1989**

Received a telex from Prof. Sazanami, Director UNCRD, Nagoya, Japan that he was pleased to invite me as a consultant to UNCRD for a period of nine months (August 15, 1989 to May 14, 1990) on a monthly honorarium of Y4,50,000 and that I will be provided with to and fro air ticket Bangkok – Nagoya – Bangkok. I felt happy. I sent a telex to Prof. Sazanami thanking him for the offer and that I have sent my C.V. by express airmail. I should think it is a God sent opportunity wherein I can make use of my sabbatical usefully in monetary, learning and writing terms.

**Sunday, August 13, 1989**

Visal and I left for Nagoya, Japan by the night Thai flight from Bangkok. A little new turn and opportunity in my career.

**Monday, August 14, 1989**

Reached Nagoya by 8.30 AM. local time. UNCRD has arranged transport from the airport to A.H. House in Hirokoji. In the afternoon, visited UNCRD and I was paid one month's honorarium in advance Yen 4,50,000/-. Met Dr. Sazanami, Director, UNCRD. He was kind to me. Briefly explained to him the outline I have prepared for the report.

Our first day in Japan. In the evening we went to one Department Store (Daaiyei) and purchased some rice and vegetables. The prices comparatively are unimaginable. For example, one big onion cost Rs. 5/-, a few ladies fingers Rs. 20/-, a cup of yogurt Rs. 60/-, and a cup of tea Rs. 40/- and so on.

On way back to A.H. House (a lodge), where we have our rooms now, we lost our way and we approached several people on the road an sought their help for directions to reach the A.H. House, but they shied away without responding to our request. Their problem was English language. At last, one passerby whom we approached took us to a nearby police station for guidance. The two police constables who had difficulty with English, finally got the telephone number of A.H. House, called them and identified the location and one kind policeman took us to the A.H. House. We were very close to it all the time. The first day ended with this minor ordeal.

The flats here are surprisingly tiny. The bathroom is like a matchbox. It is a feat to have your bath in this tiny cubicle.

**Thursday, August 24, 1989**

A feeling that how I am going to manage my report. To go according to the outline I have prepared, I have to dabble with some economic data where I feel rather weak.

To deal with Visal is a problem. She keeps a watch over my smoking. Last night had some depression felt apprehensive of my being not well.

Expenses towards vegetables and fruits are mounting.

**Thursday, August 31, 1989**

Met the Director Sazanami, at 2.30 PM. He had called Yoga also. After giving Prof. Sazanami a copy of the outline which I had prepared at AIT, I briefly explained to him what

I would like to do, primarily the report on Rural Industrialization and then a manual on training methods. His response to the later was not encouraging and in regard to the report on RI – his observations funneled down to:

1. I need not cover all the countries in Asia.
2. Statistical data are of secondary importance.
3. The emphasis should be on my approach to RI, the framework I would recommend. The last factor was emphasized by Yogo

It amounts to RI and CDP on my lines.

I do not see the prospect of visiting countries in Asia and I need not meddle with the economic analysis which has been bothering me from the beginning.

The meeting with the Director had left me with a mixed feeling that my work would be lighter on my lines comparatively strong and the prospect of continuing here appearing dim. On the whole, feelingwise it was not encouraging. The meeting lasted around twenty five minutes.

**Friday, September 8, 1989**

Visal has joined Kumar's Restaurant as a helper on hourly basis (11.30 AM to 3.00 PM). This is how she would like to avoid boredom sitting alone in the small flat where we stay now. I too encouraged her to do so.

**Sunday, September 17, 1989**

Aminta, an official at UNCRD from USA, has invited us to her home to celebrate our 36$^{th}$ marriage day. Visal has prepared for them pulihora, idli, mysorepak and pappu billalu (some food, sweets and savoury). Aminta has prepared a cake for us and presented us with a set of five porcelain plates. It is the first time in our married life, a family has celebrated our marriage day.

**Tuesday, October 24, 1989**

A touching letter from Dr. G.V. Sarveswara Rao (my colleague at SIET, Hyderabad) that he is suffering from blood pressure, diabetes and hyper ventilation and that he has been dragging on the mundane life. He is a scholar, versatile in organizational behaviour, HRM and management. He is the one faculty at SIET out of over 100, who has swallowed and digested almost all the books on psychology and management. We worked in several courses, a loving friend. I pray for his health.

**Sunday, November 19, 1989**

Srinivasa Raghavan (Post-Master General in some state in India) and Saha visited us. Raghavan gave an eye-witness account of how some goondas killed Sikhs in Delhi as a sequel to Mrs. Gandhi's assassination this day in 1984. He said that it was pre-planned and it was suspected that non-Sikhs also were involved in the conspiracy in assassinating Mrs. Gandhi, a great and a courageous personality.

**Tuesday, December 5, 1989**

With Visal left for Tokyo by Shinkansen super express. It is two hours from Nagoya to Tokyo. Seetharam (formerly a student of AIT and now a doctoral candidate at Tokyo University) and his wife with their child received us at the station. Visit to the Tokyo University Department of Urban engineering and met my old AIT colleague Taka (Dr. Takashi Onishi). He was kind enough to arrange our stay on the University Campus called Sanfo Kaikan Conference hall.

**Wednesday, December 6, 1989**

Gave a seminar at the Department of Urban Engineering of the Tokyo University on 'People's participation in Development programs. It was attended by 16 masteral and doctoral students. I felt happy that I had this opportunity of giving a seminar on the campus of Tokyo University.

In the evening, spent some time climbing and going around the impressive Tokyo Tower.

## TUESDAY, DECEMBER 26 1989

### Lahore to Delhi

At the immigration point at the Lahore airport on my way to New Delhi, the fellows were nasty, one constable coarsely asked me to speak in Urdu and demanded a police report since I am an Indian. I showed him my UNCRD identity card and told him that I am was on an official research assignment, but he threw away my identity card and nothing entered his mind, I asked him whether I could see his superior officer, but holding my passport in his hand, he kept me waiting for twenty minutes. Meanwhile, another man came, may be his superior and without giving a chance to me to meet him, this menacing constable mumbled something to him and turned to me and stamped on my passport.

Even though, now it is a democratic setup in Pakistan, the behaviour of officials at the lower levels continues to be the same as it was under the military dictatorship anit-Indian.

### Tuesday, January 30, 1990

Today is Mahatma Gandhi's death anniversary. It is paradoxical that the cause for which he died, the communal harmony discord and hatred between the Hindus and the Muslims still rages on, on the question of Kashmir. The present situation indicates that there may be another war between India and Pakistan over Kashmir.

I spent the night reading travel accounts put together by Newby – an English travel writer. In the travel accounts, one gets the details of queer behaviour of human beings in Africa. It looks savagery. I feel I am fortunate to have born in India that too in a Hindu family.

### Sunday, February 11, 1990

Kept awake till 1 AM. listening to and watching on TV

BBC program on the release of Nelson Mandela from the prison. Mandela coming out of the prison was delayed by one hour. He spent that hour with his wife Winnie, his children and grand children. Saw on the T.V., Mandela and his wife walking out of the prison's gates and his waving to the jubilant crowds and getting into the car. I was excited and I know that millions the world over who watched the program should have had the same excitement and jubilation. The rest of the night I had dreams of Mandela.

**Wednesday, February 14, 1990**

All the UN Fellows were asked to join in a meeting with a group of ten young Japanese officials of UN Bureau of the Ministry of Foreign Affairs at 16.15 today. When I went in, the Director of UNCRD, Dr. Hidihiko Sazanami asked me to sit next to him saying that I was the senior most man. We were to briefly tell the group the kind of work we were doing at the UN centre. The briefing of the officials started with me and I told them what my report was about.

After everybody's turn was over, one member of the group raised a question referring to my report on rural industrialization, how the question of environmental protection was taken care of in the process of industrialization in developing countries. I answered the question and I think it was satisfactory.

**Wednesday, March 7, 1990**

Sri Ramana Brahmam has come to my rescue. In the afternoon the Director Sazanani called me and Yogo has also joined. The Director has approved my visit to Jakarta and Seoul from March 25 to April 17 and he has also agreed to my getting the report typed at AIT and the fee per page 1 US dollar. I felt happy over this later Enomoto came to my room and informed me that the Director has approved my visit and the typing arrangement. May be Enomoto did not know that I met the Director already and that I knew about the approvals. Any way I am thankful to Enomoto.

Now I have to organize my visit and speed up my report.

**Thursday, March 8, 1990**

Reading a book now – 'Sindbad Voyages' by Tim Serein. It is very interesting with graphic details of ship building and the description of the workers from Minicoy Islands.

**Friday, March 9, 1990**

Prof. Kitimura, Kyoto University met me this afternoon to discuss and get some clarification on the Panchayati Raj set up in India. Earlier, I have suggested to him to visit NIRD. He did it last month or so. He invited me to visit his department in Kyoto University and give a seminar and 26 – 27 April.

**Sunday, March 11, 1990**

By chance, when I tuned the transistor, it was Moscow. Normally, I do not listen to Moscow, and since it was on Leo Tolstoy, I kept listening to the last part of it.

Tolstoy, while traveling on a train felt suffocated in the cigarette smoke and came out on the platform and caught pneumonia. The stationmaster discovered that it was Tolstoy and took him to his home and there Tolstoy lived for six days. He passed away on November 7, 1910. Amazingly, the quotation of that day (November 7, 1910) of Tolstoy runs as follows:

Life is a dream
Death is waking up

Leo Tolstoy, one of a very few that nature has bestowed as a gift to the entire mankind.

In the night listened over VOA (Voice of America) to a program on the National Poet Robert Frost, his voice, his readings, his poems. I should say that I was lucky to hear Robert Frost recite his famous (to me) lines:

> The woods are lovely, dark and deep
> I have promises to keep
> And miles to go before I sleep
> And miles to go before I sleep

The above lines were copied by Jawaharlal Nehru on a sheet of paper and left it on his office desk on the night of May 26, 1964, the last day of his work for the Indian Nation. On the following day he passed away. We do not know, whether Nehru had a premonition of the end of this mortal journey and how apt are the lines of Frost in respect of Nehru.

**Friday, March 16, 1990**

Felt sad, that an Iranian born British journalist Bazoft (I am not sure how his name is spelt) was hanged by Iraq on charges of spying for Britain and Israel.

I wonder what would be the future of Islam and Islamic nations! Religion should faster peace and harmony but its product now is violence and death. The primitive so-called savages appear to be wiser than some of the religious groups who may be called savages with modern technology.

**Sunday, March 25, 1990**

Checked out of Indra in the morning and moved to Subhang Hotel (US $ 48 per day). Lunch at Indra. Babar had a van his brother-in-law Adi driving. In the morning Alie came to meet me with his little son.

After lunch they took me to Indonesia in Miniature Park and the museum. It was terribly hot throughout the day. A rich cultural heritage and the variety too.

In the evening called the Hyderabd number 26 38 19, but the operator here told me that the woman who answered the call refused to call Visal. Then I called Pandu and told him to inform his mother that I was ok spoke to Jeji and Kumar too. I was shocked to hear that the monthly salary for Koes and people of his level even with a master degree is only $ 50/-. Amazing, how they manage their life. This fact is totally opposite to what I had thought of. Koes is staying with me in the hotel.

**Saturday, March 31, 1990**

Visit to Seoul-South Korea. Jakarta to Seoul. Reached Seoul by 8.30 PM. My old student Kang and an old SIET participant Shin met me at the airport. I felt happy that I met Shin after ten years.

**Sunday, April 1, 1990**

Kang took me on a tour of the Olympic village park and the stadia, a vast complex and gigantic structures and later to Lotte World Department Store, Folk village, a kind of museum, depicting the culture of the Koreans who are a branch of Mongolians. He bought for me a leather bag, a shaver and an Olympic tie-pin. He drove me around the vast city in his new car. It was an opportunity to have a glimpse of Seoul which is next to Tokyo in size.

**Thursday, April 12, 1990**

Reply from C. Krishna Reddy who is 70 now. He writes of his family, his mother passed away last year at the age of 102, one daughter Prabhavati passed away, another daughter padmavati widowed and he and his wife stay in the village Rachavaripalli. He writes that he feels lonely. An endearing friend.

**Monday, April 30, 1990**

Shimamura is the secretary to Dr. Sazanami at UNCRD. All through my stay, she has been helpful and kind to me. Today at 5 PM. She came to my seat at the UN Centre and took me to her house for a light supper. She and her husband live in a flat. They have no children. It is the only Japanese family that invited me to their home.

**Monday, June 4, 1990**

Received a folder from UNCRD and their impressions right from the Director Sazanami and the staff, their wishes about me are touching.

**Wednesday, July 11, 1990**

Received from M.C. Mittal one set of the Valayar study. Felt happy and excited on seeing my three volumes the Valayar of South India :

1. Society and Religion.
2. Culture and Economy
3. Sex and Divorce

Karl, Kisoe Sheng, Hiran etc congratulated me.

**Wednesday, October 17, 1990**

In India, and the Hindu communities and families I know are very strict in terms of their food, while eating that it is not contaminated by touch, that is the other person using his hand while he is eating or use the spoon he is using to pick up any food item from the main dish. The concept 'engili' in Telugu or 'echchai' in Tamil does not find place in other cultures.

On invitation I joined Kin (a visiting Professor from South Korea) to lunch. Poor Mrs. Kin has prepared some vegetable and I forced down a little. I could not stand their habit. They dip and collect food (curry for example) with the same spoon they have been using for eating. They have no concept of 'engili'.

**Monday, October 29, 1990**

Throughout the day until Kutta arrived from Bangalore

in the evening, I have been simply thinking of him only. On arrival at Don Maung airport Bangkok, he told me that he did not have any anxiety over the flight from Calcutta. Kutta is very sympathetic of his mother and there is nothing impossible for his mother. Kutta is intelligent and practical.

**Tuesday, October 30, 1990**

Kutta kept talking and putting questions to me till 1 AM. I could not get sleep until 3 AM.

Kutta has several Gods. He told me last night that he started with Lord Krishna when he was a small child. Later he moved to Jesus and after some time shifting to Siva and now in his words "Now Daddy, I worship the whole family : Siva, his consort Parvathi, son Ganapathi and the snake too. He has brought with him an ink drawing of Ganapathi done by himself and now it is in the room fixed to the wall where we sleep. He tells me that he should see Ganapathi when he wakes up in the morning. I feel happy to listen to Kutta. He speaks of Gods, philosophy, language and people's behavior. He is an endearing sweet.

**Thursday, November 1, 1990**

While on our evening walk on the campus of Thammasat University Kutta told me that he likes trees. "Daddy, I like trees, because they need not move about from place to place. They do not quarrel with each other and they have no problems". The tenor of his talk went on thus.

In the night, Kutta wrote and read out for me a beautiful piece on his mother. He writes well. He has mature thoughts, but the problem with him is, he is hypersensitive and volatile, gets angry fast. On one hand I like Kutta's ideas on life and God, but I am unable to stand his non-stop talking and questions and hypersensitivity. I think, he is sent to me by God. He says that I am like him, instead of the other way, (Kutta came to Bangkok to stay with me for some time).

**Friday, November 2, 1990**

In the night Kutta wrote and read out for me a beautiful piece on his mother. He writes well. He writes well. He has mature thoughts, but the problem is, he is hypersensitive and volatile, gets angry fast. May be god has sent him to me to give peace.

**Thursday, November 6, 1990**

Kutta says that he has been praying for the entire family and after 14th November (the day the second child to Pandu is expected) there will be one more member in the family, and he has to pray for the new comer also.

Since Kutta joined me at AIT, Bangkok, he has been cooking for both of us. I never thought that Kutta could cook this better. He knows several recipes. When Kutta was an infant I used to think and wish that I should eat the food prepared by him. Kutta is doing it now. This afternoon, he sat in my class (master of science group) for one hour along with the students and he also did the risk – taking exercise. He is quick in understanding, sharp and intelligent).

**Wednesday, November 14, 1990**

It is Jawaharlal Nehru's birthday and the second child to Pandu is also born today at Tirupathi. Kutta had a big task now choosing a name for the new born. Tentatively, he calls the new born (baby girl) MUNNI. (It is confirmed now) Kutta's problem, as he tells me is to have a name for the newborn, in order to include the child with the name when he offers prayers to God for its well-being.

**Friday, November 16, 1990**

Prof. Sedagopan, IIM, Kanpu, on secondment to AIT for one term by Government of India is a simple and scholarly man and an expert in the field of computer software. Hs wife

Chandra has also joined him here on the campus. On the eve of their departure to India after his secondment was over, Prof. Sedagopan and his wife prostrated before me seeking my blessings. I was touched by their respect to me. I wished them all happiness and pleasant living.

**Wednesday, December 19, 1990**

As fixed yesterday met Mr. Gunther Tharun, Chief of CDG, of Germany, at AIT. He briefly explained to me the job that I have to do – editing of a training manual on small business development, without entrusting the material (MS) to me and signing the agreement, he simply signed a cheque for two lakh Baht and handed it to me. I could not believe the trust and confidence he has in me. Mr. Tharun has taken me as a consultant. It is God's grace. He told me not to tell of this consulting to any one at AIT, for, people may feel jealous of me. When I shared this with Kutta, he felt happy.

**Friday, February 1, 1991**

While traveling for Bangkok from Bangalore, Kutta gave me two small photos of Rama & Sita and Hanuman in one and Ganapathi in another. Kutta as my mother is concerned about my health and peace of mind.

**Monday, March 4, 1991**

Improper sleep. In the dream I saw Narasing, brother and R. Subramanyam (appeared in his youth) all in white dress. Mentally, most often, I live with brother and Narasing.

**Monday, March 11, 1991**

I am thankful to Dr. Yogesh Atal, Regional Advisor for Social and Human Sciences, UNESCO, Bangkok for his foreword to my first volume 'The Society and Religion of the Valayar of South India'. Today, presented to Dr. Atal a three volume set of my Valayar study at his office.

**The Valayar of South India**

Vol. 1 : Society and Religion
Vol. 2 : Culture and Economy
Vol. 3 : Sex and Divorce

The three volumes comprising 950 pages published by Inter-India Publications, New Delhi, (1990).

**Tuesday, April 16, 1991**

Received a letter with a copy of the review of the Valayar of South India, from Dr. Damodar Tripathy, Deputy Advisor, Plan Co-ordination Section, Planning Commission of India, New Delhi. He has reviewed my three volume study on the Valayar of South India for the Kurukshetra journal. Dr. Tripathy is a development economist and his review has economic orientation. He compares my work with that of noble laureate Gunnar Myrdal, author of Asian Drama, though the canvas as he says is different. He calls my work of monumental quality blended with quantity and he calls the author of this work a master story teller. I felt elated and extremely happy of this encouraging and highly appreciative review. Throughout the waking hours I had a pleasant feeling about my work on the Valayar.

**Friday, April 19, 1191**

In the afternoon, called Dr. M.S. Swaminathan (Madras). Fortunately, he was available. He told me that he has already sent his foreword to my book 'Rural Development : Problems and Prospects', under publication by Inter-India Publication, New Delhi, and mailed a copy to me. He speaks high of the book.

**Sunday, April 21, 1991**

I rarely visit and make use of the library. Today just visited the AIT Library. I felt happy to find my three volume study on the Valayar of South India on the shelves of the library.

It is a fine feeling to see your books in the library of an institute where you are a faculty.

**Tuesday, May 7, 1991**

Received a letter from Prof. Christopher Benniger informing me that he received the books, (the Valayar of South India). He calls the work monumental. He had sent the money to account with SBH.

**Tuesday, May 14, 1991**

Received the anxiously awaited foreword from Dr. M.S. Swaminathan. In the foreword Dr. Swaminathan commends my work. It is OK.

**Wednesday, May 22, 1991**

Shocked to hear over BBC in the morning at 6, that Rajeev Gandhi was killed yesterday evening at SRI PERUMBUDOR. It was by a woman suicide bomber from Sri Lanka, a Tamil. She offered him a bouquet killing him and others instantaneously. Emergency was declared and elections postponed to June. On hearing the news felt uneasy and giddy. I lived to see three generations of Nehru's family, Nehru, Indira Gandhi and Rajeev Gandhi. No more Gandhi's in India.

In the evening a condolence meeting was organized by the AIT, Indian Association. I was asked to preside over the meeting. I spoke a few words – the tragic killing of three Gandhi's : Mahatma Gandhi, Indira Gandhi and Rajeev Gandhi. All through the waking hours it was Rajeev Gandhi in the mind.

**Friday, May 24, 1991**

By now (6.10 PM Bangkok time) the mortal remains of Rajiv Gandhi, a great son of India would have been cremated a tragic moment in India's history. I pray for his soul and for his wife and two children.

**Sunday, June 2, 1991**

By today, I am completing 38 years of service, beginning my appointment as a Gram Sevak (Village Level Worker) on June 3, 1953. This service is besides my two years service in the State Bank of Mysore, Head Office, (1948-50) I have been in service for about 40 years. God helped me all through.

**Saturday, July 6, 1991**

It was interesting to read excerpts in the Illustrated weekly on India by Gandhiji : Gandhiji says that the first sloka (hymn) in the Isopanishad or Essavasya Upanishad will sustain Hinduism, even if every other scripture perishes. The meaning of this sloka runs as follows: that Iswara or God pervades the whole world and we should reach the state of realizing the 'Paramaatma tatva by offering the fruit of all actions to Him alone. I like Gandhiji's views on Hinduism, Gandhiji, a giant among mankind.

**Saturday, July 20, 1991**

Started reading 'Guide for the prefixed' a basic book on the mystery of life by Schumacher.

**Monday, August 5, 1991**

Felt happy and jubilant when I received a copy of my book 'Rural Industrialization, Small – Scale and Cottage Industries in 'Asia' published by the United Nations Centre for Regional Development (UNCRD) Nagoya, Japan. The book is the fruit of my intensive work for nine months as a Senior Research Fellow at the UN Centre.

I find the book with excellent get up and with a beautiful foreword by the Director Dr. Sazanami.

I feel rather shy to talk to people about my books. In a span of 13 months between June 1990 and July 1991, five books of mine have been published. All God's grace.

**Tuesday, August 6, 1991**

Wrote a letter to Prof. Sazanami, UNCRD thanking him for publishing my working paper on Rural Industrialization, Small Scale and Cottage Industries in Asia.

**Wednesday, August 7, 1991**

Received a touching and moving letter from Kutta. I shed tears on reading the letter. He writes that his stay with me at AIT, Bangkok for two months last year was the happiest period for him until now. The following message touched my heart.

"Dad when you feel lonely think that I am with you"

He is like a God to me. God bless him in his studies and with a long happy life.

**Friday, October 18, 1991**

On Friday 18$^{th}$, we had the betrothal, ceremony for Jiji. The boy's side (Krishnamoorthy) comprised 30 people, they came in two jeeps. The prospective bridegroom is from a village called Ramapuram, near Gurramkonda, Vayalpad Taluk.

They were five brothers. Number two passed away a few years ago. The eldest Redeppa is the Sarpanch of the village, another is an M.Sc., B.Ed. a teacher, another brother a framer and Krishna Moorthy is M.A., B.Ed.

I just said hello to Krishnamoorthy and shook hands with him. All the invitees had lunch prepared at Pandu's.

**Friday, November 1, 1991**

Prince Philip, Duke of Edinburgh was conferred today a honorary doctorate by AIT in a special ceremony; though there was invitation, I did not go for the ceremony, because, we were expected to go in lounge suit or in national dress. I don't like formal dress. Around 3.30 PM, Babu and I saw the prince (British) while, he was leaving the campus.

**Monday, November 11, 1991**

Received a fax from one Ms. Lyne Paquette, Donor Liaison Office from Dhaka, Bangladesh that I have been selected as a consultant, as a part of an evaluation mission. The consulting job is in February and March 1992.

**January 31 to March, 1992**

During my visit to Bangladesh on January 31, until I finished my consulting work for the Netherlands International Development Co-operation (NOVIB) or call it Donor Consortium, I have not made daily notings. Here is a brief. At Dhaka stay at Rosewood Guesthouse, Gulshan, food was fine. The eight member evaluation mission consisted of Colin Reef,. (Britain, leader) Janice Jaggins (Britain), Roger Young (Canada), Mario Ganuja (EI Salvadar) Stanley Gajanayake (Sri Lanka), Ellend Sig Valden (Norway), Cliff Village (USA). My part of the consulting was 'Institution Building'. Visited some villages in the districts of Narsingdi, Jessore, Pabna and Natore.

Lyne Paquette, the DLO was nice. Colin as a leader of the team was a failure. He played games and tricks.

Met F.H. Abed, the Executive Director of BRAC (Bangladesh Rural Advancement Committee) presented him two of my books : Rural Development; problems & Prospects and Rural Industrialization, Small-Scale and Cottage Industries in Asia. Abed is an institution builder and a very imaginative constructive worker and able administrator.

**Tuesday, May 12, 1992**

In the morning shared my feelings of disappointment with Hiran. He told me Weber ploted against him also and Hiran called weber as vicious and poisonous man.

**Tuesday, June 2, 1992**

Today attended to an interview at UNESCAP, Bangkok.

The committee that interviewed me comprised the chiefs of eight divisions. The interview was for one hour (9 AM to 10 AM). I did fairly well. The consulting work is to design training programs for the staff of ESCAP.

**Thursday, June 11, 1992**

Miss Reieth, Personnel Officer, ESCAP informed me over telephone that I am to be taken in as a consultant for the entire month of August and may have to visit ESCAP once in this month to meet and discuss another consultant who will attend to the first part of the job.

**Thursday, June 25, 1992**

For the third time, since I stopped talking to him Weber greeted me good morning. I did not respond. Later on Kioe Sheng who is the acting Chairman met me in my room and asked me about my incommunicado with Weber. I told Kioe Sheng that I did not like to talk to Weber. He raised the question of Weber being on Rajan's committee and myself on India's. I told Kioe Sheng that there was no question of either of us dropping from the doctoral committee. It is clear that Weber has talked to Kioe Sheng about my not responding to Weber's greetings.

**Saturday, July 11, 1992**

Just an idea of a new book flashed in my mind. Mini Biographies or unforgettable characters, especially covering the village folk and some interesting characters that I have come across in life. I pray that God should grant me some more years of life, so that I could accomplish my planned writings (it was subsequently published under the title Diversity of life livened by Individuals).

**Tuesday, July 21, 1992**

Received a letter with the agreement copy by fax from ESCAP Suwit Habananda, Chief, Personnel Section. The consulting is for one month August 3 – September 2 1992 and the gross fee offered is US $ 6500/-. Signed the agreement and faxed it back to ESCAP. Rather a Chellenging job. God's grace.

**Friday, August 14, 1992**

I have to be at ESCAP at eight in the morning. I get up at 5 AM and with a lift on the car of Roger's wife, reach the nearby railway station – Chiang Rak, from AIT, from there travel by train to Sam Sen station and from there walk upto UNSCAP in Bangkok City.

Today I would like to record the indifferent attitude of Thai towards dark complexioned, especially Indians. I could find a narrow space between two hefty Thai in the compartment. One, on my right was sleeping and the fellow on the left was reading some book. The left fellow did not budge an inch and both of them were sitting spanning their thighs indifferent and insensitive to the non-Thai. It is a bit difficult to describe these people. They are physically fair, handsome and beautiful, well dressed, good in organizing cerrmonial things, influenced by monarchical, regal and royal traditions and Buddhism, well regulated hierarchy, across the entire administration, but their behaviour towards non-white, non-Thai is far below civilized behaviour. They admire the white Euro-Americans and they are considered as angels. Most disgusting.

**Wednesday, September 9, 1992**

On my calling Ms. Rieth, Secretary to the Chairman Mcgregar (Chief of Staff at UNESCAP) told me that she has gone through my report and it is excellent and Mcgregar appreciates the idea of sensitivity training and that they are sending my report to New York (Hqs) and that they will mail the cheque towards my fee, on the approval of the course I have designed for the staff of ESCAP, is found to be excellent.

**Tuesday, September 22, 1992**

Received a cheque for $ 1,64,450/- being the honorarium, for my one month consulting for ESCAP from ESCAP. Felt happy.

**Saturday, October 24, 1992**

For nine years now, this is the first time that I am present in India for Deepavali.

I witnessed/heard massive cracking of fire works.

**Monday, November 30, 1992**

In the morning I met Khun Nipon with copies of NIC's letters and that of president. North's letter to NIC authorizing him to use my services as a resource person in CEC courses. Nipon was kind and he told me that there will be no problem for visa extension and ordered that I should declare my income for tax purposes. Conveyed the visa question to NIC. We felt relieved of the problem of visa.

**Monday, December 21, 1992**

With pain I have to record that Siva is a born liar. He cheats and hoodwinks people, his friends and his teachers with lies. He is finished with me.

**Wednesday, December 23, 1992**

The last but one working day for me before my retirement at AIT. The Finance Department has paid me resettlement of 10%, home leave encashment, salary for December 1992 Baht 2,81,597. Besides, received a cheque for Baht 1,109,133 dated 24/12/92 being my insurance saving fund for my nine years of service. I am thankful to God.

**Thursday, December 24, 1992**

Today is the last working day for me in the division. There is a strange and to me an interesting phenomenon. Excluding my two year stint in the State Bank of Mysore in Bangalore, I joined as a VLW (village level worker) on 3/6/1953 and virtually retiring on 24/12/1992. When we add up the joining date and retiring date, it is my favourable numbers 3,6,9,12. It struck me this evening while I was on my evening walk. I am alone now. Visal is in Bangalore. God has helped me all these years in my studies, career and in my publications.

My night fare consisted of a few pieces of papaya, two oranges and a glass of milk.

**Saturday, February 27, 1993**

I am afraid that Siva would cheat me by not giving me the full diskette in respect to participatory Rural Development. He is a liar. He told me that he would leave for India tomorrow, since his visa expires this Tuesday. He is a drifter. If he fails to handover the disk, I will be losing one year's labour.

**Saturday, March 13, 1993**

Shocked to learn that Dr. Y.S. Rao Regional Advisor, Forestry (FAO) and his mother were killed in a hotel yesterday in Bombay in a bomb blast. He and his mother were on their way to Los Angeles to see Rao's grandson.

On my return from India on February 22, I called Dr. Rao and he told me that Gautam, his eldest son was blessed with a son and that he was leaving for the States. I congratulated him and he asked me to meet him at FAO on his return and that he would introduce me to the Rural Development Advisor for possible consulting.

Dr. Rao, an amiable, affectionate, kind and a scholarly man became a victim in the serial blasting in Bombay, suspected to be the heinous crime committed by some Muslim fundamentalists. Only today, (in the morning) I have checked and assembled all the chapters on Participatory Rural

Development is Asia : A Critical Analysis. With Rao's permission, I have included in the forthcoming book his paper entitled 'People's Participation in Upland Development'. Dr. Rao has been endearing friend to me since I came to Bangkok in 1984. Rao will ever live with me and in my forthcoming book. I pray for his soul

**Tuesday, March 23, 1993**

Finished reading the marvelous "Notes from the Dead House" by Fyodor Dostoyesky, the great Russian author of 19th century. It is a graphic description of life in jail in Siberia. He was confined to jail for four years. It is a great piece of literature. I am thankful to Babu, who has purchased this book.

**Thursday, April 8, 1993**

Attended the memorial service conducted for Dr. Y.S. Rao at FAO office, Bangkok. High tributes were paid to him. I wrote in the book I expressed my condolences to Mrs. Uma Devi Rao and Gautam (Rao's son).

**Friday, May 21, 1993**

Nic has no regard for value of people. He is a business man to the core. He borrowed my ESCSP report on training and instead of asking me to write the proposal on training, he has asked Mrs. Susselo to do it on environment. She would largely copy the course I have included in my ESCAP report.

**Sunday, August 8, 1993**

After lunch Hunuma took leave of me. Babu accompanied him. Hanuma is a nice gentleman. I like him. Wish him all the best.

**Thursday, September 9, 1993**

It has been a long dream for me to meet Bandala Ramaiah, my senior at the Pachaiyappa's College, Madras, often I used to recall the lines from his poems in Telugu, depicting the misery of a mother who cannot feed her child being in extreme poverty and the emaciated bullocks of a scheduled caste farmer which cannot pull the plough. While I was in Punganur, I mentioned about Ramaiah to a teacher. He told me that Ramaiah was at his native village close to Punganur. The teacher took me to that village. By the time we reached his house, he was on a visit to a relative's. I waited for him for a while and when he entered the house, I did not recognise him and on my enquiring some family member as to when we can expect him here. He said he has just now come and he is there. Then I greeted him and mentioned my name. Neither he could recognise me nor has any memory of me. He is 68 now, his face darkened, and he is affected with some skin disease. He briefly shared about his writings and that he was awarded D. Litt by the Mysore University for his poetical work on Basava of 12$^{th}$ Century. It is in Telugu. He has retired as Professor of Telugu from the Mysore University.

To his surprise and to the surprise of his family members I quoted a few lines from his poems published in the college magazine in Pachaiyappa's. The substance of the lines is as mentioned above. In Telugu, the lines and the meaning are poignant and touching. I met Dr. Badala Ramaiah after 42 years.

**Thursday, November 11, 1993**

With deep sadness, I record that Janakamma of our village passed away today. The message was conveyed to all the village people who are in Bangalore. With the passing of Janakamma, the romantic saga of her has passed away along with her. Her husband has passed away ten years ago. All members of her family died earlier. She was the last to leave.

In her youthful years, she has been a person of consequence. She had nearly two decades of her romantic life, but was faithful and devoted to her husband. She was known as a black beauty in her youth. It is alleged that she had affairs with several persons in our village.

I always associate her with Jasmine, Vallimalai Shrine, and shrines of Narasimhaswamy and Anjeneya, near Sholinghar. She was regularly visiting these shrines with a prayer that she may be blessed with a child. She died childless. Once she answered an elderly man in the village, on his asking her why she goes in for extramarital affairs, she answered the old man without any qualms and with all frankness that her husband when he does his coitus with her and when he lies on her, he weighs so light like a cork and that she does not get the feeling of consummation.

Her last days, I understand were ridden with difficulties for food and other minimum basic requirements. Govind, a close relative took her lands assuring her that he would take care of her, but it is said that he has neglected her. I remember when I saw her last in the village and enquired of her wellbeing, she just smiled and moved away. She looked to me as a solitary person dragging on with her life.

**Sunday, January 9, 1994**

Paramacharya Sri Chandresekharendra, the Sankaracharya of Kanchi Kama Koti Peetam passed away yesterday at 3.20 PM. A centeranian (1884 – 1994) at Kanchi. I had a long wish to have his darshan, but had a vision of the Acharya in a dream.

**Thursday, June 8, 1995**

Read a feature article about the Huli tribe of Papua New Guinea (PNG) where they value human hair for using as headgear. They dislike women and consider them as debilitating sources of man's prowess.

**Monday, June 19, 1995**

Started reading Huston Smith's The Religions of Man

which gives an account of principal religions of mankind. Finished reading the chapter on Judaism and half way through Christianity. Wonderful Jesus.

**Saturday, May 27, 1995**

I remember, it is on this day in 1964 that Jawaharlal Nehru passed away. It was on the eve of Narsing's Marriage. Brother I were in the village. On the same day, brother and I went to Sholinghur to purchase some items for Narsing's Marriage. A mourning state of the entire town of Sholinghur is vivid in my memory now after 31 years. Nehru a great son of India.

I remember my brother and Narasing. It is impossible to think that they are no more with me.

**Thursday, January 18, 1996**

A shocking news that N.T. Rama Rao passed away at 4 AM. today in Hyderabad, after a massive cardiac arrest. A great actor and a brave, sincere politician. He will be remembered for generations.

**Friday, January 19, 1996**

While watching on the T.V., the mourning and people paying their respect to N.T. Rama Rao, while Lakshmi Parvathi, sitting by the side of the body of NTR, wailing all through, I pointed out to the people around me that wailing of Lakshmi was not genuine and she was rather acting. Later when the body was taken to the cremation ground, it was reported that Lakshmi Parvathi was chased away from the cremation place.

**Tuesday, January 30, 1996**

In the morning I was so surprised and very happy to see Saroja D/o. Lakshmayya of Gajalapalli after 48 years. She was brought here by Abba (Krishna). She said she came to see me. I used to remember her. Often she looks old with grey hair resembling her father's mother Ragamma.

**Thursday, February 1, 1996**

After several years visited S. Venkata Rao at his residenc. He introduced his son and a daughter who were with him at the time of our visit (SSP and Krishnamurthy were also with me).

While we were at Venkata Rao's, Nemali Lakshmi, Narayana Rao arrived there with one of his daughters. He did not recognise me, S.V.R and I waited for a while and then I mentioned my name to Nemali. He hugged me with all love and affection. We were meeting after over 30 years. I was touched by his affection for me. His daughter told me that just four days ago Nemali Rao mentioning about me to his daughter. From Venkata Rao's, he dropped us at Jeji's.

**Saturday, June 1, 1996**

Dr. Neelam Sanjeeva Reddy passed away today in Bangalore. He was 83. I have physically seen only two presidents of India : Dr. S. Radhakrishnan and Dr. Sanjeeva Reddy.

**Wednesday, July 10, 1996**

One sad news brought to me by Visal that Mohananga popularly known by his nick name Gandodu Passed away in the village yesterday. He was the youngest of three brothers Bangaru, Govindu. The elder, Bangaru passed away some years ago and Govindu, left the village (he was a victim of leprosy) and never returned. Nobody knows, where he went and whether he is alive or dead.

Mohanaga was my classmate in the primary school at Diguru. He had a beautiful smile, shy, still I remember though it was over 55 years ago. The way he used to hold the slate is fresh in my memory (5$^{th}$ class). He had a fine hand writing. I used to think of him often. May his soul rest in peace.

**Tuesday, July 30, 1996**

Another heartening thing that relieved the anxiety of all is that Kutta completed all his papers and now he is a B.Sc (Computer Science) graduate.

Visal Joined Jindal. Mani came and spent around 4 hours.

**Sunday, September 1, 1996**

The marriage between Baby and Krishna took place today on the campus of Loyola College, Vijayawada. I pray for the welfare of Baby and Krishna.

**Monday, September 16, 1996**

It is our 43rd marriage anniversary. It coincides with Vinayaka Chrathurthi. Kutta was the chief in preparing and doing the puja to Ganappa. In the evening Visal sought my best wishes as usual. She has invited some of our relatives and treated them with what she has prepared for the puja.

Babu called in the morning from Bangkok and wished us a happy marriage day. He told me 'Dad I have a request to you, I would like to marry in ensuing December and I feel lonely". I assumed him and wished him all the best for his marriage with Sanjana, the main problem is Visal. Hope she would reconcile with Babu's proposal.

**Wednesday, October 2, 1996**

It is Gandhiji's 128th birthday a great soul and I should give in the Bhagavad Gita sense Gandhiji was an avatar.

**Thursday, October 3, 1996**

Sad to learn over the radio that Dr. Nagappa Alva passed away today. He was ninety. Way back in 1957 when Dr. Nagappa Alva was practicing medicine with his clinic in the Kempegowda Road, Banglore, I was his patient for one and half a months. He treated me well, with all kindness and softness. I do not remember the amount he charged for the treatment, it was a moderate amount. At this time I was working as a village level worker in former Renigunta Block with my headquarters at Tiruchanoor near Tirupati. One of my classmates introduced me to Dr. Alva for the treatment. The problem was, back sprain caused by wrongly lifting a bucket with full of water in the bathroom. I pray for Dr. Alva's soul.

**Wednesday, December 4, 1996**

When I went through my diary of 1964, I overcame with a kind of helpness feeling that I am not able to recall the details and identity of some persons who figure in my diary, though at that point of time, they have interacted with me. It is so puzzling and painful for the loss of memory.

**Friday, January 10, 1997**

On invitation from Dr. Ramesh G. Tagat, Director, Maharishi Institute of Management, Bangalore and on the approval of the National Registrar, New Delhi, joined MIM as a Professor-cum-Consltant at a monthly salary of Rs. 14,000/-. The salary I cossider as secondary and I am happy that at last I got my position and designation as a Professor, which was denied to me at AIT and the main culprits there were Karl Weber, Pama, Gajendra Singh and President Alistair North.

I am thankful to Dr. Tagat. I will be teaching the MBA students, both junior and senior.

God's grace.

**Monday, January 20, 1977**

Spent a larger part of my time with Dr. Ramesh Tagat. It was useful and I enjoyed listening to him.

Presented to the MIM – Bangalore library through Dr. Ramesh Tagat the following books authored by me :

1. The Valayar of South India (3 Vol.)

   (i) The Religion and Society.

   (ii) Economy and Culture.

   (iii) Sex and Divorce.

2. Rural Development : Problems & Prospects.
3. Rural Industrialization, Small-Scale and Cottage Industries in Asia.
4. Small-Scale Industries in Bangladesh.
5. Participatory Rural Development in Asia : A Critical Analysis.

**Wednesday, January 29, 1997**

I began my course Management and Organization today for the first year MBA students. I should say it went well. It is a highbred course with American Professor's tape and my teaching and coordination.

It is a significant day for me. Today I got my name card printed with my designation as Professor. In the Long Journey, today I have reached my destination in a sense. Ramana Brahamam.

**Wednesday, March 19, 1997**

In the evening along with Visal visited Veerabhadra who was in a coma state at Mallya Hospital. Touched his feet and prayed for his speedy recovery. May be this was the last time I saw him alive.

His wife Guramma, my childhood playmate was also sick. When I met her in the hospital, she held my hand firmly. I have special affection for her. God help recovery of both.

Later Visal (though I was with her I could not get in) visited the wife of one Venugopal brother of Bhagya) who has attempted suicide drinking some bat poison.

**Friday, March 21, 1997**

Sad to record that Veerabhadra passed away at 8.20 PM. Today, just 1 hour and 40 minitus ago. He was a affable gentleman. I always remember his smiling face especially his large nose. I attended his marriage in the village and I deeply feel for Guramma, my childhood playmate.

I pray for Veerabhadra.

**Friday, May 30, 1997**

Dr. Janis Langstaff, Faculty in-charge of Human Resources Management (HRM), Maharishi University of Management, Fairfield, Iowa in the fax to Ramesh Tagat, Director, MIM writes about me as follows:

Dear Dr. Tagat :

Thank you for having Professor Setty to teach the HRM course. He is superb, well organized, an excellent facilitator, good communicator and a great example of a leader.

Further, Prof. Langstaff has expressed her appreciation for my poem, 'THE COSMIC ORCHESTRA'. I composed this piece a couple of years ago and I thought that the poem may interest her and enclosed a copy of it along with other papers to her.

**The Cosmic Orchestra**

The Stars that Twinkle

The Sun that Blazes

The Earth that Trembles

The Moon that Shines

The Winds that Blow

The Seas that Pulsate

The Sky that Sends Forth Thunder and Lightning

The Languages Spoken

The Musical Notes Produced

By the Members of the Cosmic Family

All Unrestrained

Effects Soothing and Bewildering

An Eternal Flow of Light and Sound

A Cosmic Orchestra

Unceasing in its Play

While the Conductor is the God Supreme

**Thursday, July 24, 1997**

Sad to learn from NRC that Gurappa of our village passed away today at the village at 5.30 PM. I tried for taxi to reach the village to pay my last respects to him, but could not get one. When I met him at the village earlier alongwith Baby and Visal I thought that was the last time I was meeting him. During this visit, Baby arranged special puja to the deity in the village shrine and sought Gurappa's blessings. On that night, I touched Gurappa and greeted him. Gurappa was solely responsible for the construction of and regular puja to the deity (Sriram) at the village. The shrine is at the head of the village on the western side. Gurappa took personal care of the shrine. He will be remembered so long the shrine exists in the village – almost for an eternity.

**Thursday, August 14, 1997**

Visit to a book fair in Bangalore. Purchased 'Walden' of Henry David Thoreau, Lives of Great Scientists and Sankaracaharya's 'Vivekachudamani'. I enjoy reading Thoreau the transcendentalist. Way back in 1950's I used to carry a copy of Walden in my bag during my visits to villages as a Village Level Worker. In course of my discussions I always feel like referring to or quoting some idea from Thoreau and his friend Ralph Waldo Emerson from his 'Conduct of Life'.

**Wednesday, August 20, 1997**

With a feeling of guilt and a sense of remorse I record that Visal's mother T. Lakshmamma passed away today at 8.15 PM. It was a peaceful end. At the last moment Visal, one Venkataramanappa (father of Kusuma) and I were at a jewellery shop in the Highgrounds area. Visal was helping Venkattaramanappa in purchasing some jewels for his daughter's marriage. While we were at the jeweller's, Kutta called us and asked us to return home immediately. Kutta was the last person to give some milk to Visal's mother before she passed away.

I used to call her and refer to her as MIL, short for mother-in-law. She was unique, a loner, independent of spirit and of strong will. I knew that she would contract cancer because of her years of chewing of pan (betel leaves with areca nut and tobacco) and using snuff. I stopped communicating with her some three years ago, when she scolded Jeji "your eyes should be pierced". That enraged me. I feel bad about it.

Informed Babu, Baby, Krishna of her death. Babu as a philosopher said that his grandmother was sage-like and had a peaceful end.

**Sunday, September 14, 1977**

It is an instance of great expectation and terrible disappointment. I came in contact with Dr. Sedagopan when he was seconded by the Government of India to AIT, while I was there. During the same period Kutta stayed with me on the campus. When Dr. Sedagopan's wife joined him at AIT, Kutta became friendly with both of them and Kutta used to explain preparation of some recipes to Mrs. Chandra

Sedagopan. This was the nature of contact for Kutta with Sedagopans. They used to express a lot of fondness of Kutta.

Today Kutta and I visited Sedagopans at the campus of Indian Institute of Management, Bangalore, where Sedagopan is a Professor in computer related courses. On our meeting them, they started sharing their experiences and life in USA and about Computers and Internet. Since the computers reign the world today, anyone who is an expert in the field is reckoned high and enjoys a special status. Kutta aksed sedagopan whether he could help him (Kutta) with a job since he is a graduate in computer science.

Sedagopan simply brushed off Kutta's request saying that he did not know much about Kutta and simply expressed his inability. The wife and husband who live by themselves, only two constituting the family have no sentiment, no emotion and no helping tendency. To me, they appear as mechanical beings. Kutta who has been thinking until now, that he has been very endearing to Sedagopans, was surprised and taken aback by their response. Even though Sedagopan was not in a position to find a job for Kutta, the casual and matter of fact way the request was treated, has hurt Kutta.

**Saturday, October 18, 1997**

Manipulative behaviour of Dr. Ramesh Tagat. He tries to please the students and in the process antagonises the faculty. The case in question is Prabha without discussing with me Tagat tries to arrange outside faculty to teach Prabha some topics under HRM (which I could do). For a long time I and Viswanath shared our feelings and impressions on the manipulative behavider of Tagat.

**Sunday, December 28, 1997**

Often I do not pay attention to details and ask for details and also the curiosity to know mundane details of people and their affairs is far less. This seems to be the influence of my attitude towards life which is transitory. You will leave this physical world and lose memory of your physical existence. The following instance indicates my casual interest in some events.

Earlier in the day, Visal asked me to attend the last rites of a person. I failed to ask her the identity of the deceased person and thought that the last rites were of Thippigonolla Chengalrayadu, our villager, long back settled in Bangalore. At 12 noon Visal dragged me to the choultry where the rites were being performed. I did not enter the premises of the choultry and sat outside. I saw several of our villagers who have come for the ceremony.

Rites over, I saw Kumaraswamy, his two brothers Eswar and Raja and Eswar's wife Saraswathi inviting people to lunch at the choultry as part of the ceremony. I could not make out how Saraswathi and her family were inviting the visitors to lunch, since they were not closely related, to Chengalrayadu who I thought was the person who died and for whom the last rites were performed. I asked somebody there how Saraswathi is related to the family which was performing the rites. The person told me that the rites were in respect of Chandra, the youngest brother of Kumaraswamy. Though I was there for the ritual for over one hour I had no idea that it was Chandra who has passed away and the last rites were for him.

So far as I know, Chandra has led a tragic life and an unattended and solitary death. He was the youngest son of Kaviah. I saw him some two years ago after nearly 30 years. Though he has been in Bangalore, right from his birth and his brothers too in Bangalore, he had very little contact and interaction with his brothers and their families. He has taken to drinking. It was alleged that he used to allow his wife sleep with other men, take money from them and use that money for drinks. Sometime ago, his wife has deserted him and eloped with another man. For a few months before he passed away, his feet were swollen with pestering and oozing wounds but he did not seek help or shelter at any of his brothers'. During his last days, he stayed in a park day and night. Nobody knows how he has managed his food and how he lived alone in the park. Only after he passed away a lonely death, unattended, somebody who saw the dead body and identified the person reached the information to his brothers.

Since I came to Bangalore in 1996, I saw Chandra a couple of times and enquired of him briefly. I remember him as a slim, optimistic and soft spoken person and devoted to his little daughter. I learn that his little daughter (6 years old) is being taken care of by her mother's mother. One can imagine the future of this child. I don't think this child will have any contact with her paternal uncles, their children and their families. A sorrowful state.

**Thursday, January 1, 1998**

Last night it was fun for SSP and Kutta on the dawn of the new year. These two fellows danced to the cassette music beyond mid night.

Babu, Baby and Krishna called from US and wished us a happy new year.

## MARCH 31 1998

**Kutta Arrived from Holland**

Visal and I received him at Bangalore airport. He told us with all excitement that he had a very pleasant time for over two months in Holland. He had an opportunity of visiting Germany, Belgium, Paris and London. He enjoyed the snow fall. We are happy that he is back.

**Monday, June 15, 1998**

In earlier centuries and decades the scheduled castes

especially Mala and Madiga (cobblers) were hesitant and reluctant to reveal their ethnic identity for fear of segregation, discrimination, humiliation and illtreatment at the hands of upper castes. This was during the period, which lasted for several centuries when caste hierarchy was rigid and casteism reigned supreme, but now since there is reservation for political, economic, social and educational benefits, the members of the scheduled castes declare their identity. The case at present is one Krishna Madiga who is on hunger strike in Andhra Pradesh demanding categorization of subcastes among the scheduled castes. It is interesting to note the changing norms and social values.

**Wednesday, October 7, 1998**

Sad to note the demise of Harry Miller in Madras yesterday. He was 75. He died of heart failure. For several years, prior to my leaving for Bangkok in the beginning of 1984, I have been a regular reader of Miller's articles in the Indian Express. His articles especially on Snakes and Irulas were highly interesting and informative. I remember to have read that he has adopted an Irula boy some 20 years ago.

Today's obituary on Miller mentions that he was a British, came to India in 1947 and settled in Madras. He was awarded OBE (Order of British Empire) by Queen Elizabeth II. Harry Miller was an interesting writer. I enjoyed reading his articles.

**Friday, November 19, 1998**

I have a mixed feeling – a little happy and overall feel sad that Babu has to go in for registered marriage with Sanjana at San Francisco in the morning time (California time) night in India. I had dreams that Babu's marriage was to be celebrated on a grand scale. Somewhere around 10 P.M (IST) Babu called and wished him best wishes and also wished Sanjana. I could not wish heartily since Visal as an antenna was watching me. She swears that she will have no contact with Babu, if he married Sanjana. Babu told me that on coming to India, he will plead with his mother and if she agrees, the marriage may be celebrated in a traditional way in Tirupati.

**December 17–24, 1998**

Babu informed his mother that he had already married Sanjana. She became hysterical and behaved like a possessed a person and used very derogatory language against me and other children too. She is dead against Babu marrying Sanjana. Earlier, I was apprehensive that she would commit suicide, since she has been threatening and swearing that she would end her life, if Babu marries Sanjana.

I don't feel that I can have any interaction with her. She is adamant, illogical unreasonable and highly egoistic.

I pray to god for a peaceful end to Babu's alliance with Sanjana.

I understand the feelings of Visal.

**Thursday, January 7, 1999**

Sad news, though it was expected JayaLakshmi, wife of Naga and daughter of Devanamma Prasad away at CMC this afternoon she has been suffering from heart trouble and after operation, she passed away. She was fifty.

Visal and I left for the village by bus. We left at 9.30 P.M. Reached Chittoor 2.30 P.M and village by 5 A.M paid our homage to Jayalakshmi on seeing her dead body.

**Friday, January 8, 1999**

In the entire course of my life I have never seen a funeral in the village so largely attended by people from some villages and they thronged the funeral. Some dozens of garlands of roses adorned the dead body of Jayalakshmi. I expressed my condolence to Naga. 'He wept like a child'.

**Sunday, January 17, 1999**

K. Namasivayam of Veermangalam village about seven Km. from our village was my classmate for six yeas from 1st to 6th Form at A.P.M. High School, Sholinghur. The last time we met each other was in March 1948 after our SSLC public exams. I think our class comprised some forty students including five girls. Since 1948, of several of my classmates I have been thinking and dreaming of meeting Namasivayam for the past fifty years. Whenever I visited my village and chanced to meet old schoolmates, I used to enquire the whereabouts of Namasivayam. I was told that he was in Madras and no more details. Meeting him remained an unfulfilled wish and dream. Last Friday while attending the funeral of Jayalakshmi W/o. Nagabhushanam and D/o. Devanamma at our village, met Balasubramanyam of Peddaramapuram who also came for the funeral, on my enquiry, he informed me that Narasivayam has passed away last year. A chilling information. His image of 1948 remains in my memory. He was mild and soft spoken. I wonder whether our spirits would meet.

**Monday, March 1, 1999**

Kumar returned from Maldives. It is two years, since he left for Maldives. Visal and Pandu received him at Bangalore bus station. As soon as he came he touched my feet and shed tears. He looks fine and confident. He has earned some modest amount during this period.

**Wednesday, April 28, 1999**

Earlier Dr. Cargal – of CMR Institute of Management studies has invited me to teach a course of 3 credits on 'Indian Society'. Today I gave an introduction to the course. I am providing the students (MBA) my own article on caste and urbanization published 31 years ago.

While at the institute Achar showed a book written by Professor S.C. Dube. 'Indian Society'. Of course I am familiar and quite conversant which the matter that Dube has dealt with. When I looked at the back side page of this small book, felt sad that Dube passed away in 1996. I should have done my Ph.D. under Dube. I met him once in Trivandram. Some time in 1969. I read his book 'The Indian village' a great sociologist.

**Saturday, May 22, 1999 – USA**

Visit to Devon, a suburbon area, a composite shopping centre of Indians, Pakistanis, Jews and Bangladesis. Had a glimpse of Michigan lake and Skyscrapers. The structures are inspiring, fine roads and the whole thing appears as a park.

**Saturday, May 29, 1999**

USA is a gifted country. Apart from natural resources, she is blessed with, aggressive and competitive and technologically supervisor human resources. Her whole environment is maintained so meticulously. Other countries may have to emulate several of the principles and practices of USA.

**Wednesday, June 9, 1999**

The idea of God – Truth. Though it is not knew, it struck me this evening that the idea of God – Truth – Reality may be likened to the trunk of a tree and the various faiths – religious orders are the branches and the multifarious, sects within the main religions are the sub and sub branches and all supported by the trunk, but having grown tall and having moved in various directions, they are not able to visualize the parent trunk and these religious sects and sub sects fight with each other though all are in search of God/Truth. It really looks funny.

**Monday, June 21, 1999**

Completed reading Darwin, interesting and enlightening

book an the fact of evolution and origin of species and especially of genetic inheritance.

**TUESDAY, JUNE 26 1999**

**Religion:**

- It is a kind of software to know the unknown.
- It is mainly a set of codes of behaviour and principles governing individual and group conduct.
- It is mainly sociological and psychological, not much to do with spiritual things.
- How religion has divided people and cause for enmity, wars and continuous communal riots.
- Religion makes people sane and also mad.
- Religion is a divisive force.
- There could be only one Reality, one Truth, and one God, but people's imaginations and images appear different.

**Thursday, July 1, 1999**

Started reading very witty and humours Gilbert Principle by Scott Adams. Though this book is there back home in Bangalore purchased by Babu I didn't touch it thinking that it dealt with management a dull affair.

**Tuesday, July 9, 1999**

Yesterday I read a special report in the July 1998 issue of Reader's Digest (US Edition) on Osama Bin Laden, Islamic terrorist, intoxicated with his Islamic faith looks at all non – Islamic people as anti Islamic. In the case of Muslims, the religion has become a weapon and added to their faith. Money has added to their ferocity and terrorist activities. I have been thinking of their faith and the faith led behaviour and the instances show that my views and thinking are right. To me it appears that religious dogmatism would be a force to be reckoned with, as it has been in the earlier centuries. Only a section of people in the Islamic faith indulge in such irreligious activities.

**Saturday, July 24, 1999**

Babu took us to a Sequoia Forest for sight seeing. We left at 2 P.M and returned to Bakersfield by 10 P.M To and fro distance is 265 miles. Nearly one hour drive was on narrow, sharply winding roads. The peak of mountains is 12500 ft. we could reach only half of it. It is an area where you have the convergence of three towering mountains, with deep valleys.

We had the opportunity of seeing giant Sequoia trees towering nearly 300 feet. One ancient tree named General Sherman, height 270 feet, circumference 103 feet, diameter 30.2 feet. One has to strain to see the peak of the tree. It is recorded there that the tree is said to be oldest surviving tree 2281 years. The forest with rich Sequoia trees of several generations in terms of the girth and age of the trees present a panoramic view, a scene to be seen and admired the might of the nature.

One fallen and lying on the ground an ancient Sequoia is so wide that the cars could be driven on it for a few feet. It looks like an ancient fallen angel, something that could be likened to the sleeping Kumbakarana of Epic Ramayana. One Sequoia which has fallen down in 1936 is so large it lies across the motorable road and they have cut part of the wood under it belly and know cars pass underneath the lying tree.

A spectacle to see.

**Friday, July 30, 1999**

Babu took us to YOSE MITE national park area - water falls it is gigantic mountain area. Two giants things one animate, the wooded forest and the inanimate towering mountains. Night stay at Oakhurst Hotel.

**Saturday, July 31, 1999**

Sight seeing mountains and wooded trees – extensive and vast fields under cultivation totally mechanized. Stay in a hotel at San Francisco.

**Sunday, August 1, 1999**

Visit to Golden Gate Bridge and viewing the Bay and touching the Pacific Ocean water. USA is a fortunate country with the gift of nature and labour and intellect of people. She appears invincible.

Returned to Bakersfield from San Francisco by 11.30 P.M. Babu all through in this three days covered 840 miles. He felt very tired driving long distances. God help him.

**Saturday, August 8, 1999**

Last day stay in Bakersfield. Since Visal refused to meet Sanjana, Babu is undergoing terrible stress, but he is great and he has infinite patience and tolerance. I admire him.

**Monday, October 4, 1999**

With deep sadness, I note here, R. Jaganath my contemporary, may be one year younger to me passed away last night. Visal and I we were able to reach Chadarghat just on time, a few minutes before cremation. He worked as a bill collector in Andhra Electricity Board. He was a soft, mild man. His three sons were not efficient and especially the eldest one, Shunmugam has been a liberal spender and has incurred loss and lost several lakhs of rupees and as result Jaganath had to sell his house at Subramanayanagar, Bangalore.

Mani, Jaganath and myself are childhood school and playmates.

I pray for his soul.

**Sunday, October 31, 1999**

Call from Babu, Baby and Kutta. They are concerned about my cough and health. Krishna, Baby, Kutta and Chinbi will be flying to San Francisco to be with Babu and Sanjana on their 1st marriage anniversary.

God bless them.

**Tuesday, November 30, 1999**

Just now at 9.15 PM, heard over AIR that eminent social anthropologist M.N. Srinivas has passed away. I and Babu had an opportunity of meeting and talking to him, I think in 1987 at ISEC, Bangalore. I read his Religion and Society among the Coorgs, Remembered Village, on caste etc., he became famous by his coining Sanskritization, Indeginization, Westernization and secularization. He looked like a sage in the field. I should say that I was his indirect student. May his soul rest in peace.

**Saturday, February 2, 1999**

Received orders from the Director General of Doctor Marri Chenna Reddy, Human Resources Development Institute of Andhra Pradesh, Sri. P.V.R.K. Prasad offering me a possession of consultant in the field of training for a period of two years on the following terms.

1. Monthly fee Rs. 25,000/-
2. House rent Rs. 5,000/- per month
3. Provision of transport
4. Telephone at residence and office

It is unique opportunity for me. It is all God's.

**Wednesday, December 31, 1999**

The last day of the year. I should say that the year 1999

was favourable for our family. Krishna got a job in Hewlett Packard in Chicago Baby and Krishna have reached Chicago and Baby also was selected as an associate of HMP and he will join his job in February. Baby in USA is in a new job and Kutta was selected by a Dutch Company and he will leave for Holland next week and Krishna Murthy joining MIM for M.B.A and above all, in my case, Joining MIM as a Professor the destination I have been aspiring to reach. It is all God's help.

**February 18 to March 24, 2000**

I resume this dairy after a lapse of five weeks. When Visal and I left for, Hyderabad on February 17th evening, I forgot to collect my diary.

Joined Dr. MCR HRD Institute of Andhra Pradesh on February 8. For 9 days the Institute arranged our stay at Manjeera Guest House. Took a flat at Motingar, Plot No. 26, 4th floor D-3. Visal left for Bangalore on 28the February.

Contacted some old friends, nearly after half a century. contented A. Achyuta Naidu over telephone. Find it different to stay alone. Intensive thought over Babu and Crystal and Kutta.

**Sunday, March 26, 2000**

It is a significant day in two ways. In the morning I waited for the Director General P.V.R.K. Prasad, IAS at his chambers he came at 8.40 AM he greeted me and immediately suggested that the participatory rural development may be published in two ways

1) A full length book to be distributed to all the libraries in the state and

2) Just important guidelines in brevity to be provided to the field workers as a field and operational guide in respect to Janamabhoomi in rural development programmes.

When I asked DG whether I would be introduced to the Chief Minister Nara Chandrababu Naidu, he said 'Yes' that he will introduce me to CM at tea time. The DG asked me to attend the meeting conveyed by the CM. It was attended by all the Ministers, Secretaries, Deputy Secretaries and Head of Departments. The CM came at 9.00 AM. He spoke for 1 hour on how to plan and achieve progress. His speech was excellent with wealth of ideas and guidelines. The speech was followed by questions. The CM answered all the questions superbly.

At the tea – break (11.30 AM) the CM went to the DG chambers and I got in informing the gun holding security to inform the DG inside that I was so and so and later the DG came out and signaled to me to come inside and introduced me to the CM briefly giving my background. The CM listened to me attentively and told me "I have to discuss with you at length and will be happy to write a foreward". To the book to be published.

I shook hands with him. I felt happy. Now my work begins preparing the MS.

First time in life to meet a Chief Minister.

**Monday, March 27, 2000**

Visited Prof. EG. Parameswaran at his flat near Taranaka in the evening after a gap of 22 years. Both of us were happy to meet after so many years. He was very appreciative of my self growth. His love for me was solid. He looks old, but active. He lives alone and a widower. His one daughter he told me was in USA as Asst. Professor married to an American. His second daughter Deputy Accountant General is in Mumbai and his son runs some business in Hyderabad.

I mentioned the name of Dr. K. Harigopal to him. He got wild and called Harigopal a scoundrel, a rascal and a person not to think of. Harigopal was a student of Prof. Parameswaran and his advisor for his Ph.D. I learned from Prof. Parameswaran that Dr. M.S. Swaminathan is his first cousin. EGP a great humanistic scholar and teacher.

**Saturday, April 1, 2000**

On reading R.K. Laxman's autobiography – Tunnel of Time I wrote him the following letter.

From

Dr. E.D. Setty,
Consultant,

Dr. MCR HRD Institute of AP
Road No. 25, Jubilee Hills,
HYDERABAD – 500 033.

To
Sri. R.K. Laxman,
Political Cartoonist,
Bennet, Colemann & Co., Ltd.
O/o. TIMES OF INDIA
Dr. Dadabai Naoroji Road,
BOMBAY – 400 001.

Date: 01.04.2000

Dear Sir,

Namaskara.

I don't have adequate vocabulary to congratulate you on your swift and fast moving '**Tunnel of Time**'. While I was going through your autobiography I felt I was sitting in the Simkhansen Train in Japan. When I was a UN Research Fellow in Japan I used to travel by this train from Nagoya to Tokyo. I have gone through your autobiography when I was alone in Hyderabad and your book kept company. On several occasions while running through your fast moving narrative

I laughed to myself to the point of shedding tears. The language especially the adjectives used to describe or portray the satirical side of the persons or the events are very unique. Your autobiography is part historical. At some places I felt like reading Sir Conan Doyle's **Sherlock Holmes**. I have been a regular reader of the Times of India. The first thing that I see is 'your cartoon'. And gaze a while at the constant common man. Years ago I used to enjoy the cartoons in the Punch and the cartoons of David Low and James Thurber. While going through your autobiography, the areas where you mentioned about your stage fear and that your have been in your school and college days, a back bencher, I found that I too had such inhibition and nervousness to begin with and all through my school and university days I have been a back bencher. And with this similarity I thought that you must be a Scorpio (born between October – November). But this idea that you may be a Scorpio was contradicted by your skill in repairing time pieces, again I thought that you may not be a Scorpio. I have gone through some of your 'YOU SAID IT' series and even before you explained about your interest in drawing crows, I started admiring the poses and moods of the crows that were drawn for this book. Before I read your book I used to imagine how you select a particular event, theme, or a person for your daily 'You Said It' and I have detailed description of how you go about it and switch on your mind to arrive at the satirical cartoon for the day. Your autobiography provides some glimpses of other nations you have visited and the cartoonists you have met. While going through your work at some points I felt and thought that you are something like an X-Ray penetrating into the behaviour of people. Your common man has become something immortal.

There are several sentences in your narrative which are rather poignant and quotable quotes. I would like to mention one or two such sentences "largely politics was the profession of school drop-outs; I observed that politicians were the most durable among the human species. They were tough, impervious to humiliation, failure, defeat, insults, shocks. They lead a conscience – free existence, hungry eternally for power even charged with corruption, fraud and murder" (P. 184).

In a number of references the identity of the individual, the name and station of the individual are not revealed in the narration. For example, while reading the book, I was looking forward to know as to who was your childhood friend HK. There may be reasons for not disclosing the identity of some individuals including some of the cartoonists. I felt sad when you mentioned that HK has passed away.

I really feel happy that I had the opportunity of reading your interesting autobiography. And it is really a current of ideas, impressions, anecdotes, comments, descriptions all infused with satire and humor.

With warmest regards,

Yours sincerely,

**(Dr. E.D. SETTY)**

**Consultant**

On receiving the above letter Sri. R.K. Laxman wrote me a letter which I reproduce below.

THE TIMES OF INDIA GROUP

April 15, 2000

Dear Dr Setty,

Many thanks for your letter of April 1, 2000. I was overwhelmed by your reaction to my book "The Tunnel of Time". In fact, you induced me to read my own autobiography with certain objectivity to note the finer points which, perhaps the writer is unaware of. Appreciation from an enlightened person like you encourages me to pursue my inclination to write more seriously.

With warm regards,

Yours Sincerely,

R.K. Laxman

Dr. E.D. Setty
Consultant
Dr MCR HRD Institute of AP
Road No. 25, Jubilee Hills,
Hyderabad – 500 033

**Wednesday, April 5, 2000**

Ugadi of Vikram year. As planned visited Dr. P. Sambasiva Rao, now a faculty at the REC Training Institute. He and his wife were happy to see me after nearly 20 years. I was in a sense responsible for Mrs. Rao's job in a bank. They are blessed with two sons. Spoke to them. While we were there Dr. Rao called P. Narasimha Reddy, my old friend. He joined us. We hard lunch including the driver Sattar.

From there we went to Mr. P.N. Reddy's flat. His wife could not recognise me. Their three daughters were in front stage when I saw them. Last one has grown up now. The eldest is married.

**Saturday, May 6, 2000**

Call from Kutta and Babu. Kutta spoke at length. Received e-mail from Kutta. One full page, beautiful language and ideas. He says he is with me and prays for me. His description of black African American women especially of their dress is an excellent description.

**Tuesday, May 9, 2000**

I was rather surprised when the D.G. Sri P.V.R.K. Prasad

came to my room and introduced me to one Mr. Yugandhar gentleman whose name I did not get in full. It is the same Yugandar (IAS) whom I called in Bangkok when he was in ESCAP, but his tone was rather matter of fact. Yugandar told me that he is organising some training for the disabled and asked me whether I could be of some help. Sri Prasad has already briefed Yugandar about me. I referred to people's participation then I mentioned to him about my book and when he wanted to see it I brought the book and showed it to him, he noted the address of the publisher. He spoke with the usual high airs of an IAS man.

**Wednesday, May 10, 2000**

A mowing, touching and a beautiful letter from Baby. His language is fine and he says that from 1st June be is moving in his position to systems and work in the same building where Krishna works. He writes about Chinni and as a mother he feels proud of him. He feels proud of his father and Erram family. If need be, he will later help Suresh.

On reading his letter I shed tears several times and could not control my emotion.

Brilliant Baby.
God be with him.
Just 2 biscuits and 2 bananas for dinner.

**Friday, May 19, 2000**

Received a beautifully drafted letter, from Kutta, which I consider as a piece of literature. He writes that he is proud of being his father's daughter. I find in him a future writer. I feel happy about him.

**Sunday, June 18, 2000**

At 4 PM. Kutta called from New York and told me that today is Father's Day and he wished me. He told me that he was leaving for San Francisco and would stay with Babu until he gets placement. He is sweet.

**Monday, July 3, 2000**

Prepared a draft on Master of Arts in Good Governance with details of core courses specialization courses, and with credit breakup and bibliography submitted it to the Director General of Dr. MCR HRD Institute of Andhra Pradesh.

**Tuesday, July 18, 2000**

My work earlier for UNESCAP in Bangkok has come handly for the courses I have to designed now and slightly modified six courses to be submitted to the D.G. Yanadiah typed the material so well.

**Wednesday, July 20, 2000**

Designed and submitted the following six training programs to the Director General.

1. Attitudes and Human Behaviour.
2. Management of Motivation.
3. Management of Change.
4. Management Relations and communication.
5. Formulation and Implementation of Projects.
6. Project Management.

**Friday, July 28, 2000**

I should record here the kindness and noble nature of Sri. P.V.R.K. Prasad, IAS, the DG of the Institute. In the noon I met him in his room and asked him whether he has looked into the courses I have designed as required by the Board of Governers of the Institute. Then he picked up the file I submitted and showed it to me and said that he is keeping it to go in detail. While taking leave of him he said with his natural beaming smile "whenever you are free come and sit with me. The (the faculty) are hesitant to meet you and request you to take any courses they coordinate by virtue of your age and seniority". He shook hand twice. I felt elated and thanked him.

**Sunday, July 30, 2000**

Met a Achyuta Naidu after 50 years. He looks old with faltering speech almost immobile owing to constriction of limbs and fingers. He narrated his experience as VDO and then his college studies doing B.Sc (Ag.) and working as agri officer and retired in 1986. He did not ask anything about me. May be he was informed of my job, movements or he was not interested to know about me. I felt happy that I met a friend after half a century. He was staunch admirer and follower of Prof. Goginani Ranga and P. Rajagopal Naidu.

**Tuesday, August 8, 2000**

A shocking information from Visal through the letter of S. Alexander addressed to me to Bangalore address that R.S. (Dr. R. Subramanaiam) has passed away. It is not clear whether it was in India or USA. He was a great intimate friend of mine. He was my teacher and colleague. He was a great scholar and effective teacher. His wife Godavari was endearing to Visal.

I pray for his soul.

**Monday, November 20, 2000**

In the absence of Krishnamoorthy crystal is so much attached to me. He sleeps with me. Some times I bathe him. He is very intelligent. He learns anything, so fast. He is one and a half year old and he speaks a few words Tatha, Ammamma, Nana, Daddy, Anna, papa, Neellu I never saw him afraid of anybody.

**Tuesday, December 12, 2000**

Along with Yanadiah met the Planning Secretary A.K. Parida and handed over to him the MS (Model for Peoples Participation in Janamabhoomi – Rural Development) along with DG's note to the Chief Minister. He read my draft of foreword by the Chief Minister Nara Chandrababu Naidu (this foreword refers to Janamabhoomi written by me). He pruned it eliminating my name as the author. He made a shorter version of the foreword minus mentioning of my name. Later I met Ranadeep Sudan special secretary to CM handing over the MS to him and told him with an emotional tinge what Parida has done. He assured me he would see that my name will be there in the CM's foreword. I do not now how to describe Parida. I think of him as a hand tool.

**Wednesday, December 20, 2000**

An idea to attempt a book, which struck me while returning home in the car from the Institute.

"Resistance to change in Diverse Fields Across Centuries".

- Religious
- Ideological
- Economic
- Social
- Technological
- Territorial
- Political
- Administrative

**Tuesday, January 30, 2001**

Received communication from the Dean of Osamina University to the effect that the UC & OU Prof. & C. Reddy has nominated me as a Co-opted member to the Governing Body of P.G. College (Autonomous) Secunderabad for a period of two years. Felt happy. It is all god's. I owe this to Prof. Vakil. Called and thanked him.

**Sunday, February 11, 2001**

For many years now I have been thinking of the influence

of environment on the growth, development and behaviour of man and research findings mentioned in respect to genome says that heredity is the foundation and the super structural is the work of environment.

**Thursday, April 19, 2001**

In the class today (TQM in Management) I spoke on delivery service. With the analogies and examples that I shared with the participants, I sent them into uncontrollable laughter and I also could not contain myself and my laughter. I think the group enjoyed my class. Most of these were Revenue Divisional Officers.

**Thursday, May 3, 2001**

A significant day. At 10 AM the Hon'ble C.M. Nara Chandra Babu Naidu released my book, 'A Model for Securing People's Participation in Janamabhoomi'. Rural Development at Dr. MCR HRD Institute of Andhra Pradesh. As per the suggestion of DG. P.V.R.K. Prasad, the CM handed over to me the first copy. Later the CM put a shawl on my shoulders and while doing so, he said that "I was thinking of 'Neeru – Meeru' you have to write on that" I thanked him the opportunity he has given me for writing the book. I was congraluted by several people. I felt happy. I owe the whole thing to Sri. P.V.K.R. Prasad.

**Sunday, May 6, 2001**

I do not know whether Visal will change at all. I have not come across any person male or female with this kind of adamancy and rigidity. She cares more of her views, the illogical stand she takes not even showing any emotional feeling towards people especially in case of Babu.

God should help her.

**Sunday, June 17, 2001**

Crystal's birthday. Kutta has arranged delivery of cake,

sweets and toffees through Banana. Pandu has arranged cake separately. Visal, Pandu, Tiny were busy throughout the day. After seven Crystal's birthday cake was cut. He did as guided. I presented him the book A Journey Through Time. Which is dedicated to Crystal, SSP and Mahi. I was overcome with emotion when I did it. Some 60 students of Krishna Moorthy attended the function. It went off well. A memorable day in my life.

**Saturday, June 30, 2001**

Very distressing news. Today 2.00 AM Dr. M. Karunanidhi was dragged from his house in Chennai beaten by the CB CID Police who pounced on him as starved wolves. His nephew Maran and another Union Minister Balu were also arrested. This is the heinous act of Jayalalitha. Her days are very close. She will not continue as CM. It is law of nature.

I am touched by the way Karunanidhi was handled by the Police as Robots.

**Tuesday, July 30, 2001**

I am happy to note that based on information given me by Visal that Dr. N. Radha Krishnan my old colleague at Gandhigram Rural Institute, called her at 4 PM. Both of us felt happy that we were able to contact after over ten years. Now he is Director of Gandhian Institute of Studies and Research, Delhi, which is under the office of the Prime Minister of India. He is a nice man and a Gandhian.

**Friday, July 27, 2001**

Today I had a two hour session for an NGO group of Balram and some lady participant told me (the session was on communication) that usually they fall asleep during the afternoon classes, but this afternoon they enjoyed my class and my humor kept them awake.

**Tuesday, September 11, 2001**

An unbelievable catastrophe has taken place. Just at 9

AM the two highest world trade centers (110 floors) were blown off by two suicide planes master minded by Osama Bin Laden. The causality is said to run into thousands. As I have been thinking and telling people that there are two destructive forces in the world one communism and another Islamic fundamentalism, one could see these happening.

**Tuesday, October 2, 2001**

Today is Gadhiji's 132nd and Lalbahadur Sastri 97th birthday. On TV I saw some of the glimpses of Gandhiji recorded a year ago. It was so touching and I shed tears while watching Gandhiji, his brisk walking, his child like smile and simplicity.

**Monday, October 8, 2001**

As expected US and Britain attacked some Taliban positions in Afghanistan beginning 9.55 PM (IST). President Mushraaf is in a predicament and his life is in danger. One fanatic Osama Bin Laden has created havoc all over the world.

**Sunday, November 25, 2001**

A couple of days ago I presented to Dr. C. Kondaiah three of my books (1) A Model for Securing People's participation in Janamabhoomi Rural Development, (2) A Journey through Time and (3) Neeru – Meeru. He did not have the courtesy to thank me, may be out of jealousy. He would have felt inferior.

**Wednesday, November 28, 2001**

The CM Nara Chandra Babu Naidu released the book Neeru-Meeru at 12.25 PM at the Jubilee Hall during Collectors conference. Unfortunately the videographers were not present and three men took photos. I stood by the CM and I received a copy from him.

**Tuesday, December 11, 2001**

At 10 AM the Institute has arranged a talk by Swami

Dayananda Saraswathi of AIM Seva. The CM and his wife and several secretaries etc. were there. The DG welcomed and introduced the Swamiiji. The DG spoke excellently and Swamiji's speech was beautifully covered with humor. Most of his ideas are similar to mine, except in respect to desire. He rather does not find fault with desiring, but what is that you do after realizing.

**Saturday, January 26, 2002**

53rd anniversary of Indian Republic. It was observed with full security. India is strong. The Muslims all over the world are creating enmity to them. They should realize as they think and believe that their religion is great and only faith to be reckoned supreme, that other faiths also are great according to the respective followers.

**Wednesday, February 27, 2002**

Started reading S. Radhakrishnan's Indian Philosophy inimitable style, scholastic. He analyses with profound understanding and with authority based on his wide knowledge.

**Tuesday, May 7, 2002**

A beautiful e-mail from Baby. He writes, he read Journey Through Time for an hour and all through shed tears and he says the book is a gift to the five children.

**Thursday, May 16, 2002**

A shocking call from Pandu that he has resigned his job at INYS (Jindal). He was treated badly. He cried over the phone and Visal and Kutta called and talked to him. I asked him to resign if he had not done that so far. INYS has no human values. It is a stifling organization. God should help Pandu.

**Friday, May 17, 2002**

In a way it was a significant day. The DG. P.V.R.K Prasad

introduced me to the Chief Minister Nara Chandra Babu Naidu around 11.30 AM at the Institute. On introduction, the CM stood up from his seat and I briefly explained to him what the DG has suggested to write on, and I presented to the CM to following complementary copies :

1. The 3 volumes of Valayar of South India
2. The Journey Through Time.
3. New Approaches Rural Development.

The CM smiled and shook hand and wished me all the best. It is rather significant that an author presenting five books at a time.

**Wednesday, May 22, 2002**

Sad to note that Pairu Srinivasulu passed away, the message was passed on to me by Kutta from Bangalore as informed by Budatha. Kutta reached Bangalore this morning.

Srinivasulu died a bachelor, the last man to leave his generation. He should have been 100 years. I saw him some two years ago in the village. He was in the field on the western part of our village and I met him and gave him Rs. 20/-. He said why for me with a smile. I pray for his soul.

**Friday, May 24, 2002**

Krishna Moorthy arrived from Tirupathi in the morning.

While I was at the Institute around 1.30 PM received a shocking call from Kutta – Bangalore 'Dady I married Sujeeth today at a temple' I said, 'God bless you' and he put down the receiver. He has made similar call to Visal and Pandu too.

I felt Dizy for a few minutes. I didn't take lunch. Returned home. Visal was tense she couldn't stand this news.

I can't imagine what Kutta's life would be, where he will stay and what he would do and how our relation with him would be in the future. This child has been extremely endearing to me.

**Monday, June 3, 2002**

Today June 3 1953 I joined as VLW in the Rural Welfare Department at Madakasira, Ananthapur District. I have been in continuous service over half a century.

**Saturday, June 8, 2002**

Kutta left for Bangalore. Though Visal has been stiff despite request and continuous persuasion by Kutta after Kutta left to the hotel, Visal called him and spoke to him shedding tears and asking Kutta to come back and stay with us. Kutta purchased Pulla Reddy sweets and sent them through Veeresh, the driver. Kutta is so concerned about his parents. God help him.

**Thursday, June 20, 2002**

On the advice of B. Nageswar Rao, Visal prepared the necessary items for puja and she has invited four ladies and at 11.30 AM, we entered the new professors' quarters on the HRD campus. We were given a flat bearing numeral 12. Driver Veeresh and the newly taken attendant Mahinder helped the event a great deal. All the invitees, the driver and Mahinder had their lunch at the new quarters.

Kutta called in the afternoon and he asked me whether he should leave for US from Bangalore or Hyderabad. I told him that he need not simply beg his mother and better he leaves from Bangalore and further I told him that I am inclined to meet the person Kutta has married. I feel for Kutta. It is his own making. God help him.

I have been praying to God for Krishna Moorthy's selection.

**Sunday, June 23, 2002**

On the invitation extended by Dr,C.V. Narasimha Reddy

attended the function at the Bharatiya Vidya Bhavan. The function was arranged to inaugurate C.V.N Trust and release Dr. Reddy's book on Public Relations and Communication. It was released by Swami Alokamarthananda, President of Rama Krishna Matt at Hyderabad. His speech was fine so also Dr. Reddy's and Narendra Luther's.

**Friday, June 28, 2002**

As a member of Board of Studies of Political Science of Osmania University attended the meeting; met the Chairman Prof. Iliah and Prof. Purushotham Reddy. Suggested a course on "Good Governance". For the first time took out the car Tata Indica.

**Saturday, July 6, 2002**

My article on EDP among women in Asia has appeared in a Journal published by Jaipur EDP centre, sent to me by my old student Siddhartha who is the Director of this Institute.

**Thursday, July 11, 2002**

By afternoon Nagumomu came to my room and murmured into my ear that the Director General had signed an order appointing Krishnamoorthy for a two year period at ten thousand per month, but no idea at the moment whether it is under psephology project or at TPC at the HRD Institute itself. At last the Director General has done it, thanks to him.

**Friday, July 19, 2002**

Took Visal to my room at the Institute to receive the call from Baby. We went there at 8.30 PM waiting for Baby's call from Chicago. Meanwhile Jeji called from (Tirupathi). He spoke to Visal and I think he complained of Krishnamoothy. I have to record the admirable sentence Jeji used referring to Krishnamoorthy.

"We can motivate a person but we cannot mould him".

Jeji is sharp in English. He will never lie and he is like his father. I feel happy and proud of Jeji for his frankness and boldness.

**Thursday, August 1, 2002**

Vijayasree was/is the culprit in creating poor impression of my sessions and I have to suspect her who carried stories to Ranjana. VS is a shameless climber using the help of other people. She uses people as ladder.

**Saturday, August 3, 2002**

It is Visal's birthday. I wished her a happy birthday and many returns of the day. In the afternoon she sought my blessings. Krishnamoorthy and me are the only two wish her on this day.

Kutta has arranged delivery of flower bouquet and a cake (delivered by Banana) with happy birthday wishes to Visal, all members of the family, Kumar, PKM, Pandu, Jeji, Babu, Baby, Kutta, Tiny, Chinnakutta, SSP, Crystal, Mahi, Manu, Ammu, Sanjana and Sujeeth wished Visal a happy birthday. It was the idea of Kutta.

All the children called their mother wished her a happy birthday Babu, Baby and Kutta from USA, Pandu from Bangalore and Jeji from Tirupathi.

God bless Visal.

**Sunday, August 4, 2002**

Often I forget the name of the place where Buddha gave his first sermon. Once I am not able to recall the name, I wanted it becomes a mental torture for me. Yesterday I thought of the place of Buddha's first sermon. Once I try to recall the name, any name for that matter, I cannot divert my mind on anything else. Even if I deliberately try, it would be a futile exercise. Last night I struggled so till 3 AM, then I remembered I have noted the name in my small telephone numbers book, which I had kept in a brief. I got up at 3 AM., opened the brief and looked into the note book. I saw the name.

Sarnath near Benares, I stayed at Sarnath for a week when I attended a seminar at Gandhian Institute of studies organised by Sugatha Das Gupta from whose letter to me (January 1995) I often quote his sentence "Let us draw strength from each other". On the T.V. I watched the thunder birds and Horn bills. A wonderful evolution of life.

**Friday, August 9, 2002**

In the afternoon on my way to the quarters around 2.30 PM. two participants of Management of change training program returning from the canteen after their lunch greeted me and told me that my session for them on change was the best and all of them rated me excellent and incase of other faculty they gave them very good and good. Felt happy.

**Saturday, August 17, 2002**

In the afternoon met the newly appointed Joint Director General R. Seetharam Rao, IPS. He received me kindly. When I began introducing myself he told me that the DG told him that Setty has grown from grassroots and he is one to depend upon on training and Rao added that I was welcome to meet him at any time and I am an elderly man. I felt happy it is all divine.

**Monday, October 21, 2002**

Anmol publishing company representative and another sales agent Narender and Srinivasa Moorthy met me at the Institute. I wa happy to know from Moorthy that New Approaches to Rural Development is becoming popular. He said he handed over to Rural Development Minister Nanjappa

(Karnataka) a copy of the book. Discussed with him the possibility of Anmol publishing Reflections on Training, a Critical Guide with some changes. Moorthy said that he would communicate the idea to Joshi of Anmol.

**MONDAY, NOVEMBER 4 2002**

**Dynamics of Dalits Development**

It is Social conversion not religious. Conversion to Buddhism is only one step inside or one step outside Hinduism.

Similarly in the case of conversion to Christianity or Islam.

How can you expect a turn about in the psyche and attitude of people. Is it changing attitude.

Marketing of religion.

**Wednesday, November 6, 2002**

Visal cannot stand my handling money. She is wedded to money. For her money first and people next.

I had to blast her orally for her only concern for money. Money is her only life. It is suffocation with her.

**Sunday, November 13, 2002**

Chimbolli's daughter's Nikita's birthday. Visal and I attended the birthday. Tiny too.

Shocked and felt extremely sad to learn that Devani passed away last year. I met her during the marriage of Sriramulu's youngest son. I have been often thinking of meeting her she resembled an apple quite endearing. I pray for her soul.

**Thursday, November 14, 2002**

Chinakutta's birthday. Visal sent word to village to bring Bujja to Bangalore. Ramamoorthy brought Bujja by 4 PM.

We were about to leave to the railway station. I saw my dearest sister after over two years. She looks pale, lean, weak. It pained me to see sister in that state. Took leave of sister, Ramamoorthy & Pandu, Kumar and Tiny and Kutta saw us off at the city railway station.

**Wednesday, December 18, 2002**

Last night Kutta called around 11.30 PM and told me that he very much wanted to talk to his mother, but the mother is dead against receiving any call from Kutta. He told me that he has been suffering from neck sprain. I understand his feelings but none can change Visal. He told me that Manu dances as I used to do when Kutta was very young.

**Sunday, December 22, 2002**

The dark continent is really dark steeped ignorance we get this image when we read Frazer's Golden Bough amazing work running into 13 volumes.

**Wednesday, January 22, 2003**

Here is a brief account on field study undertaken from $6^{th}$ to $21^{st}$ January in conection with documentation of Janmabhoomi, Neeru-Meeru, Empowerment of Women and HRD Initiative. Left on $6^{th}$ morning with Yanadaiah, Satish in Tata Sumo, the driver was Ali of Akbar Travels. Visal accompanied us upto Bangalore. Visited some Mandals/Grama Sabhas in the districts of Kurnool, Anatapur, Chitoor, Nellore, Prakasam and Guntur.

Importantly visited village on $12^{th}$ and saw may be for the last time N. Sreenivasulu, Chinnabbha in their last stage. Visited village after nearly three years. Bujja looked better. At Phalaram met K. Narayana Rao and his brother after 50 years and at Sodam Varanasi Ramaswamy Reddy's wife, Annaiah, Mrs. Reddenna and B. Sambasiva Naidu, at his village near Bangarupalem and K. Neelakanta pillai after 40 years. Returned back on 21st night.

**Sunday, February 2, 2003**

A great tragedy the American space shuttle Columbia crashed before it landed in Texas. The crew of seven including an Indian American Kalapna Chawla died. A great effort of man and a great tragedy.

**Wednesday, February 19, 2003**

The Deputy Director General (Dr. MCR HRD Institute of AP) R. Seetarama Rao called me over telephone and expressed his appreciation about my book 'A Practical Hand Book on Training'. I thanked him saying that I value the appreciation from an author like him. Later Sri. Chengappa (ADG) called me. I presented him a copy of the above book and he was very happy.

**Wednesday, April 9, 2003**

Met the DG in the afternoon and told him that the centre has released. Rs. 13,30,000/- towards documentation of projects. Mentioned to him that I am doing all the five projects.

**Monday, April 14, 2003**

It is interesting to note a blend of political strategy, personal popularity and homage paid to Dr. Ambedkhar a dalit leader. After his death his name is helping the dalits. This is how history has turned into mythology.

**Tuesday, April 29, 2003**

My priority topics for writing are the following.

1. Man in search of God (since published).
2. Dynamics of Dalits Development (since published).
3. HRD for Emerging Rural Leadership.

4. Training for Rural Development.
5. Development of Entrepreneurship among Women (since published).
6. The Long Journey (Autobiography).

God help me with health and long life to accomplish the above topics in book form.

**Monday, May 5, 2003**

Very sad to now that Jayaram (of old CIET) a close friend of me and family, passed away a few days ago. He was a highly intelligent man, a marathon talker and a friendly type. He has left for his family real estate assets worth 10 millions rupees.

I will ever remember him. I pray for his soul.

**Saturday, May 17, 2003**

Visal and I left for Chennai in train 1$^{st}$ class A/c. leaving Nampally by 3.50. Right from morning as usual I had to hasten, Visal to get ready. It was a little better in 1$^{st}$ class A/c.

**Sunday, May 18, 2003**

Arrived Chennai central by 5.45 AM, Obolu's son and Raju were waiting to receive us. They drove us to the Hotel Woodlands where Gandhi was staying. Spent some time with Gandhi. They arranged our stay in the hotel.

In the evening we went to the so called reception at Kalingar Hall (I am not able to spell the full Tamil name of the place). They had some music. It was so horrible, the audio level reached skies. Some thousands of people attended the function. Gandhi should have spent some lakhs.

**Monday, May 19, 2003**

The marriage function was a DMK function.

Dr. Karunanidhi, Prof. Anbualagan, Dorai Murgan and several DMK people attended and spoke and blessed the couple Shilpa and the bridegroom. The speakers were Doraimurgan and Karunanidhi. We came to know that it was intercaste marriage, the bridegroom later we learnt from Mani that he belongs to potter community, that the girl and the boy as medical students fell in love and the marriage was as a result of the girl being firm to marry the boy.

We really feel for Gandhi, may God help him
We did not eat at the marriage function.

**Saturday, July 13, 2003**

Felt sad to know that Venkatraya Pillai, my old colleague has passed away recently. Last week I wrote him a letter and sent him copies of Neeru-Meeru and Janmabhoomi. I sent to his address from Neelakantan Pallai's residence when I visited him in January in Chittoor.

I pray for Venkataya Pillai, an able and interesting man.

**Monday, July 21, 2003**

Had a session on communication. At one point the participants could not contain laughing and so one participant asked me to stop my lecture for a while.

**Thursday, July31, 2003**

After nearly three years visited brothers. Met Yasoda, Bhaskar, Suresh and the children Rajeev, little one (Ravi) and wives of Bhaskar and Murali. They were happy for my visit. Took with me Yanadiah and we (including driver Prakash) had lunch there. God bless them.

**Monday, November 10, 2003**

When I called Purushotham, he told me that he along with Bujja and his daughter-in-law is have visited brother's and chanced to read Journey Through Time and he shed tears on reading the way I have led my life.

**Monday, February 2, 2004**

Horrible and painful sight to see cattle loaded in trucks driven for sacrifice by the Muslims for their Bakird. They enjoy killing. I think over fifty percent of the people are ignorant. All in search of the unknown narrow minded, short sighted people.

**Monday, February 23, 2004**

I felt rather helpless when Yanadaiah told me that he has resigned from the Institute. He has been with me for over 4 years and prepared 12 MSS of books and documents.

**Friday, July 16, 2004**

Called Prof. E.G. Parameswaran, usually we speak in Tamil. I enquired him of his health and he said 'Paravaille'. It is ok. Then he advised me Setty what you have done so far is enough. You should go in for some part time work, meaning not to engage myself in full time job.

**Sunday, July 18, 2004**

Shocked to see in the paper that Prof. Parameswaran has passed away yesterday. I should say it was divinely ordained, that I called him a day before he passed away. He was a great scholar and I had the opportunity for 25 years to have close contact with him. After coming to Hyderabad in 2000 met him several times at his residence. Usually we used to speak in Tamil. On my request he has reviewed my book a Practical Handbook on Training for Edutrack Journal.

Most agonizing thing I think was, he was alone when he passed away. May be, due to heart attack.

I pray for his soul.

**Monday, July 19, 2004**

Last week I sent to the new D.G. A.K. Parida four documented books with a note indicating that I was sending the books to him for his information. Today, the books are returned to me, the DG not making any note or sign on my note. May be he expected that I should have met him and handed over the books to him which I did not want to.

**Wednesday, August 4, 2004**

Received two author copies of "Clinical Approach to Rural Development". The getup is excellent priced Rs. 900/-. It is dedicated to Sri. P.V.R.K Prasad, IAS, the ex. DG. of this Institute.

**Thursday, August 12, 2004**

Sent copies (one each) "Clinical Approach to Rural Development" and "Clinical Approach to Promotion of Entrepreneurship among Women" to Dr. A.P.J. Abdul Kalam, President of India and to Prime Minster Dr. Manmohan Singh by speed post.

**Thursday, August 31, 2004**

Joshi of Anmol Publications told me over telephone that he works as a slave with the publishers and they are very mean people and do not do justice to the authors, whose books they publish. I felt sad about Joshi's situation.

**Thursday, September 2, 2004**

One Mr. Poorna Chandra Rao who is with Sri. Nara Chandra Babu Naidu arranged and I talked over telephone with Chandra Babu Naidu. I told him that I would like to meet him and present some books to him. He gave appointment to meet him at 10 AM tomorrow at his residence. All God's I leave it to Him.

**Friday, September 3, 2004**

Met Sri. Nara Chandrababu Naidu at his residence at 10.30 AM. presented him my two books.

1. Clinical Approach to Rural Development.

2. Clinical Approach to Promotion of Entrepreneurship among Women and the following documented books.
3. Neeru-Meeru
4. Janmabhoomi – Rural Development
5. HRD Initiatives in Andhra Pradesh
6. Empowerment of Women in Andhra Pradesh.
7. E. Governance

He received me well and said that he will look for some activity for me and asked me to contact him after a weak.

**Wednesday, September 15, 2004**

Received a letter from President of India Dr. A.P.J Abdul Kalam, in reply to my two books sent to him a few days ago. Here I write the copy of the letter.

A.P.J. Abdul Kalam
Rashtrapati Bhavan
New Delhi – 110004

August 30, 2004

Dear Dr. Setty,

Thank you for sending me your books.

1. Clinical Approach to Promotion of Entrepreneurship among Women and
2. Clinical Approach to Rural Development.

I have gone through the books and particularly I liked your thoughts on working with people "in your book" Clinical Approach to Rural Development. My best wishes.

Yours sincerely,

**(A.P.J. Abdul Kalam)**

I felt happy.

**Friday, September 17, 2004**

Shocked and felt sad to learn from Govindu son of Obul Setty that Pairu Goindu passed away a week ago in Bangalore through heart failure. Govindu was my first childhood friend. We grew together and played together, a simple hard working man. I feel for Sakuntala, his wife and elder sister of R. Gandhi I pray for the soul of Govindu.

**Wednesday, May 11, 2005**

Marriage of Prakash S/o. Bujja whom I call Chinnabujji. Since K. Purushotam has been made General Manager of 10B and retained in Hyderabad itself. The marriage was largely attended. It was at Raja, Rajeswar Gardens. Visal, Crystal and SSP were with me most of our large family members from Bangalore and village attended the marriage. Personally wished Chinnabujji Prakash a happy marriage.

Presented a copy of 'Journey Through Time' to NRC (Radha Krishna) spent larger part of my time with him.

**Sunday, May 15, 2005**

Ramamoorthy left for village, gave him six hundred and told him that I will send fifteen hundred tomorrow. When Visal used some mean words towards me I got wild and banged her. I got wild because she was telling him that she wants to dispose of our lands in the village. She did not have minimum principle of consulting me. Since most of the proprieties are in her name, she behaves like a dictator.

**Thursday, May 19, 2005**

Crystal by birth is mechanically minded. He is interested in examing some gadgets and asking non ending questions now for three days it is the Nokia cell is his focal point. God help him.

**Saturday, May 28, 2005**

Read a few pages in lectures on Gita by Aurobindo. High

flown language. There is beautiful balance between the language and the ideas and interpretation.

**Tuesday, May 31, 2005**

Babu called. His mother received the call and as usual she used strong abusive language towards sister and Siramulu. She does not like the above two cultivating the land in the village. She threatens either she will sell the land or entrust it to others.

**Saturday, July 16, 2005**

Today is Baby's birthday. In the morning wished him a happy birthday. I was the second person to see him on the day he was born when Visal's mother brought him from the room. I remember his tongue being slightly dark. Baby is a rationalist, is highly confidant and works as a diplomat I wish him a bright future and sound health.

**Monday, July 18, 2005**

Babu called and he had been selected as Regional Manager of a company and the per anam salary, he said may range from one lakh thirty thousand to forty thousand US. I congratulated him. He warned me not to share this with anybody. He plans to come. I asked him to reach either on 31$^{st}$ or 1$^{st}$ of August. Visal expects all the children to be present on her birthday on 3$^{rd}$ August.

**Thursday, July 21, 2005**

Very sad news just now (12.45 PM) conveyed by Pandu that Ramaiah (Sriramulu) died, that someone ran over him. It is understood it was an auto. Ramaiah was a simple and helping type. He took care of all the children. He was endearing to me. He was addicted to drinking. He bore all the problems. I pray for his soul.

**Sunday, July 24, 2005**

I called DK. Adikesavulu and he spoke around 20 minutes

with a lot of sarcastic humor. In his characteristic humorous way he having volunteered to, support the project and he will pay me some amount (he did not specify) and reimburse my travel expenses and that I could proceed with my work on Clinical Approach to Alleviation of Poverty and Dynamics of Dalits Development. All God's.

Now I can stay in Hyderabad and with a steno I can proceed with my work.

**From August 12th to 29th 2005**

I made a mistake at the Bangalore airport. I had only a brief case instead of carrying it as hand baggage; I placed it on the weighing machine and did not collect and carry it to the checking point. It created a commotion and they told me that several times they announced over the mike system which I did not hear. Later before embarking, after checked in, I some men carrying the briefcase and placing it at the exit grate. I recognized that it was mine and told them so. I had to open it and show them. Then it was put under baggage. I am losing memory and forgetting things.

**Sunday, September 11, 2005**

Fateful day. I mad a grave mistake and received a painful shock and in a sense I take it a turning point in that part of desire. The shock I cannot share with anybody except to Para Brahmam. I should thank God for this change.

**Saturday, September 17, 2005**

Baby and Krishna (as Baby told me) had a two day training in Jaipur. In the session when the participants (17) were asked to name one person whom they take as a mode, when the turn came to Baby, he told the session that his model is his father. On asking who his father, he told the class about the simplicity of his father and how he has grown from simple job (VLW) and reached UNO as a Senior Research

Fellow (UNCRD, Japan). I felt happy listening to Baby, his logic, erudition, understanding, knowledge etc. He is a wonderful child. God be with him.

**Sunday, October 2, 2005**

136th birthday of Mahatma Gandhi.

Called Sri DK. Adikeseavulu at 8.40 AM, he spoke for about 20 minutes with his usual humour and sarcasm. He spoke of the life of Mala and Madiga and Sub-sects among them. It was interesting for my forthcoming books. He said that I may go ahead and he will ask his institute in Chittoor to send some money. I do not know how much it would be and I will proceed with my work.

**Friday, October 28, 2005 - USA**

Most of the day kept silent. Nothing productive. No question of any intellectual discussion. No interesting books at Baby's. They have little time for reading. Krishna, besides his official work, spends a larger part of time with the children bathing and feeding them. These operations go in a systematic way.

**Friday, November 4, 2005**

In the forenoon along with Babu and Kutta visited Sanjana's who have arrived from US last night. I felt happy to see Erram and Ammu. I have been dreaming to see them. He is a replica of Babu, an exact print of Babu. Spoke to Sanjana's father at length, and with her mother also. Later in the evening Sanjana visited us at Baby's with Erram and Ammu. Ammu speaks English with American accent. Visal saw the children, but remained original dislike person. Kutta left for US via Kualampur. Krishna, Visal and I saw him at the Delhi International Airport. Kutta looks fine, an active and affectionate child.

God be with him.

**Saturday, November 5, 2005**

Babu called. He felt happy that I saw the children I told him that Erram looks exactly like him.

**Monday, November 7, 2005**

Along with Visal went in a taxi arranged by Baby met Kripal Joshi of Anmol Publications in the afternoon and also his colleague Srikanth. I had a different mental image of Joshi in terms of physique but he is different. He is of a medium build, a little stout and with a larger head. He received us and treated us so warmly and affectionately. Handed over to him a C.D. and a floppy of "Man in Search of God". He told me that he will get it published either by Anmol or some other publisher and added that he will see everything (books) I write, and he will get it published. A kind man. Took leave of him.

Later met M.C. Mittal. This meeting was after 14 years. He spoke some pearls of wisdom. On my asking, he gave me five copies each of 'Journey Through Time' and 'Diversity of Life lived by the Individuals'. A nice and simple man.

**Saturday, December 24, 2005**

Called Sri. D.K. Adikesvulu. As usual be was humorous and critical of the 11MPS who have been removed from the parliament. He said, once the books are printed, we shall see that they are released by Sri Nara Chandra Babu Naidu. His talk, was quite encouraging. I am thankful to Sri. D.K. Adikesavulu.

**Sunday, December 25, 2005**

Christmas, a grand elaborate ritual and entertainment.

Sad to learn that Bhanumati, a great actress passed away last night around 11.45.

**Friday, March 3, 2006**

Read in Books that changed the world, Henry David Thoreau's Civil Disobedience. It was really, I do not know how to say it, without anybody suggesting to me I picked up Walden of Thoreau and thoughts of Ralph Waldo Emerson. Some spirit has been behind me in my pursuit of reading some significant books and start writing the things which are familiar and convincing to me.

**Thursday, March 16, 2006**

M. Yanadaiah visited me. He has been selected in Group 1 written exam and he is expecting interview from 27th of this month onwards. I think he will be selected. Gave him a set of documented books and a copy of Diversity of Life Lived by individuals and suggested to him to show all these books and the other four of Anmol Publications and the interviewers will be impressed with the factor that Yanadaiah was closely associated with me the author I wish him all success.

**Saturday, March 25, 2006**

It is sad to record the demise of Chengalrayalu husband of Kamala D/o. N. Chinnabbha Setty. Visal and I attended the funeral. Saw the dead body. It was Suresh, Bhaskar, Murali and Satish took change of preparing and disposal of the body. Purushotham and close relatives attended the funeral. I understand that Chengalrayalu treated Kamala so harshly. When I informed Krishna Moorhty he said that Chengalrayalu was a sadist.

**Friday, March 31, 2006**

I called DK. Adikesavulu and felt happy he was available and when I told him that I tried yesterday to wish him a happy Ugadi, his reply to it was highly humorous and he said "that even those who have not voted for him will be calling and wishing me and so I switched off the cell". I just laughed over this observation and when I told him that I would like to spend some time with him (meaning to enjoy his humour) he said I am welcome. He mentioned that he received my letter. Hope he will send a cheque for some amount.

**Saturday, April 1, 2006**

Happy to note that Pandu is adjudged number 1A doctor at Institute of Nature Cure and Yogic Sciences and he is given an increment of Rs. 2000/-. He felt Jubilant and the children too. I congratulated him and I wish him all the best.

**Wednesday, May 3, 2006**

It is a very sad day. I just called Udaya's Trivellore office and shocked to know from the receiver that Udaya passed away last night at 2 AM of heart attack. On four days ago I called and talked to him. He said that he was on a week's leave and would arrange to send the DD on receiving the loan from the bank. The way he used to address me as Maama was so sweet and affectionate. His body was shifted to Athimanjeripet. This I came to know through Sriramulu who called me from Athimanjeripet, who went to see the body. He told me that he placed a garland on the body. It will be cremated tomorrow. Sweet and lovely Udaya. I pray for your soul.

Copy of the letter addressed to Dr. A.P.J. Abdul Kalam

To

Dr. A.P.J. Abdul Kalam,

Dear Sir,

Namaskaram, I felt like writing to you. You are personification of simplicity, humility, humbleness. I see in you John Ruskin (Unto The Last), Ralph Waldo Emerson (His essays – Conduct) and David Henry Thoreau (Walden).

I am not praising you, I know that you are beyond praise. You are a rare combination of a great scholar, scientist and statesman. You serve as a model to administration at every level.

While working on my doctoral dissertation on the Valayar of South India I stayed on Rameswaram island for 25 days in 1971 interviweing the Valayar engaged in fishing (Meenavar, Kariyor). It was a memorable stay on the island and useful and interesting data I have collected. The Valayar study was published in three volumes in 1990 by Inter India Publications, New Delhi. I understand through press, articles in news papers that you are a veracious reader. A simple man but intellectually great.

I hope you may find sometime to glance through the book that I am sending you now, Women Empowerment through Entrepreneurship Development, A Socio-economic Approach. I try to share my ideas and experience. God be with you. With Warmest Regards.

Yours Sincerely,

**E.D. SETTY**

**Friday, May 12, 2006**

Sriramulu informed me over telephone that Gandhi has been elected as MLA of DMK. I called Gandhi and congratulated him. A sad thing that Parthasaradhi of Diguru has passed away yesterday. I often quote him as an example, his attempt to speak English when we were in the elementary school in Diguru. He used to say "well go ra" meaning let us go for swimming in the well.

**Monday, September 4, 2006**

Received 5 copies of 'Man in Search of God' from the publisher, Delhi. It is an excellent get up of the book. Felt happy and called Mr. M.P. Misra the publisher and congratulated him for the excellent get up of the book and I felt happy.

**Wednesday, December 20, 2006**

Of late I have been not regular in writing day-to-day happenings, but today I felt like writing. Nearly after 52 years my VLW colleague in Madakasira Block, K. Narayana Rao called me from the residence of Surya Prakash, Bangalore. I felt happy talking to him after half a century. Last time we met was in June 1955. I ever remember him. He told me that he is 79 and I told him I am also of the same age. When I mentioned the initial to his name 'K', he was surprised that I remember his initial. I told him that I will meet him, when I visit Bangalore next time.

**Saturday, January 6, 2007**

Sad news. In the morning the son of Srinivasulu, brother of Subbanna, cousin of NRC called me that Srinivasulu passed away in the village at 3.30 AM today. He was a simple and innocent man with a smiling face, hard working man. He must have been around 85 years. I pray for his soul.

God be with him.

**Sunday, April 1, 2007**

For a long time I have not been noting down as I used to for years.

Two happy things. Akansha Publishing House, N.Delhi has published two books. 1) Dynamics of Dalits Development with a foreword by hairon Singh Shekawat, Vice President of India (Price Rs. 600/-) and 2) Clinical Approach to Alleviation of Poverty with a foreword by Charanjit Singh, Deputy Speaker of Lok Sabha (Price Rs. 1400/-) the books are of excellent getup.

A page has been added to the two books that Sri. D.K. Adikesavulu has sponsored and patronized publication of these two books.

I think, Mr. Adikasavulu is concerned and confident of my writing and so he has asked me to work on.

"Politicians in India" I told him that I would work on this and he is very eager and enthusiastic about the topic he has proposed.

**Monday, April 30, 2007**

Along with Sri. D.K Adikesavulu met Sri. Chandrababu Naidu at the party office and presented to him the following books.

1. Clinical Approach to Alleviation of Poverty.
2. Dynamics of Dalits Development.
3. Man in search of God

Felt happy, Releasing of the first two books is scheduled tentatively for 12 May in Delhi. (It did not take place as noted above).

**Tuesday, June 5, 2007**

Very sad to note that my old friend K. Narayana Rao of Phalaram (Gudibanda) passed away on May 10th. As usual I rang up his son Surya Prakash to inquire the state of cases in respect to R. Shankar and Devenamma. On calling he told me this sad news. Narayana Rao a simple and friendly man. He was my guide and a friend when I was VLW in Gudibanda in 1954 - 5. I pray for his soul.

**Sunday, September 16, 2007**

It is our marriage day. Marriage took place on September 16, 1954 in Bangalore. Today, Pandu, Jeji, Krishna Moorthy and Crystal were with us. Babu, Baby greated us. At this point of time 7 PM. Kutta has so for not called.

**Saturday, October 27, 2007**

Today is my 80th birthday. All the children have come

Pandu, Jeji, Babu, Baby and Kutta. Babu and Kutta came from US and Baby from Delhi. Krishna Moorthy and SSP and Crystal attended the birthday function. I felt happy that Brahmam survived me till today my prayers to Para Brahmam.

**Friday, November 9, 2007**

Along with Krishna Moorthy met Andhra Pradesh Assembly Speaker Sri. K.R. Suresh Reddy and presented to him the following three books :

1. Man in Search of God.
2. Dynamics of Dalits Development.
3. Clinical Approach to Alleviation of Poverty and handed over to him questionnaires (400 in No.) related to a study "Profiles of Political Leaders in India suggested by Sri. D.K. Adikesavulu to be distributed MLA and MLC's.

**Tuesday, January 1, 2008**

New Year Day. Some people especially K. Purushotham and Bujja wished me and Visal. All the five children wished both of us a Happy New Year.

For the past of couple of days going through my old diaries and marking some abstracts with an idea of publishing them in the book form under the title "YOU DON'T TRAVEL ALONE IN LIFE".

The other one which I have conceived some 20 years ago 'THE LONG JOURNEY' an autobiography.

Further I plan to attempt a book 'THE MISSING LINKS IN HRM – A CRITICAL ANALYISES'.

■■■

# INDEX